180 ICEBREAKERS

to Strengthen Critical Thinking and Problem-Solving Skills

by Imogene Forte
and Sandra Schurr

Incentive Publications, Inc.
Nashville, Tennessee

Cover by Geoffrey Brittingham

ISBN 0-86530-345-2

PRINTED IN THE UNITED STATES OF AMERICA

TABLE OF CONTENTS

PREFACE

Perk your students' interest with 180 icebreakers that cover everything from body snatchers to brain food, fables to flights, and predators to pyramids. Whether you are a teacher or a parent, you will find that these thought-provoking vignettes will increase your communication with your students. They can be used to encourage parent/child communication at home, reinforce homeschooling, or promote discussion in the classroom. As these facts lead to discussion, your students will strengthen their higher-order thinking skills while they develop an interest in the fascinating world around them. They will also learn to discuss and support personal opinions while developing springboards to investigation and communication.

Each icebreaker includes an intriguing factoid, a point to ponder, and a project to pursue. Incorporating Williams' and Bloom's taxonomies, the icebreakers address each of the intelligences and the six levels of thinking. Students are challenged to stretch their imaginations and their minds as they think of solutions to many problems such as how to reduce junk mail, save the rain forest, and encourage recycling. They use their creative abilities to write acrostics about social issues, empathize with the people on the *Titanic,* and design original artwork. These activities will promote independent thinking and will help students succeed in school and in life.

Use an icebreaker as an early morning classroom warmup, as a jump start for family dinner discussions, or as an independent project for a homeschooler to investigate and then discuss with the rest of the family. However it is utilized, *Icebreakers* will forever change the answer to the question, "What did you learn in school today?"

Acrostically Speaking _____ ICEBREAKER 1

An acrostic can be one of the most creative forms of poetry. It provides the poet with a structure for creating a poem dedicated to a specific subject and/or conveying a message of sentiment in a poetic vein. It was a favorite form of poetry used by the ancient Roman, Hebrew, and Greek cultures. The acrostic is usually unrhymed and the first letters of the lines when read vertically should spell out a word, phrase, or sentence related to the poem's subject.

Point to Ponder

Writing helps us to see what we think. How does this form of poetry help or hinder you from writing what you think?

Project to Pursue

Use a topic related to a social issue of concern to you (respect for diversity, peace, prejudice, democracy, antiviolence, etc.) to create an original acrostic.

Airplanes: The Birds of The Sky _____ ICEBREAKER 2

The world's largest commercial airplane is the Boeing 747, often referred to as the jumbo jet. It is approximately 230 feet long and 62 feet high with four engines, eighteen wheels, and 500 passenger seats. It weighs 356 tons. The Boeing 747 can reach a speed of 600 miles per hour at an altitude of 43,000 feet. In order to take off it needs a runway nearly two miles long. The first 747 was built in the 1960s and the first flight of a 747 took place in 1969.

Point to Ponder

It has been said that if God wanted people to fly, He would have given them wings. How do you feel about this statement?

Project to Pursue

Compute the length and height of the 747 in inches and in centimeters. Do the same for the altitude of 43,000 feet. Next, compute the weight of the 747 in pounds and grams. Finally, compute the total distance a 747 at an altitude of 43,000 feet could fly in twenty-four hours if it didn't have to stop for refueling.

Allowances as a Form of Income ____ ICEBREAKER 3

Income is the amount of money that a business or a person receives for doing work, selling a product, or providing a service. A person who has a job will receive wages or a salary, which are forms of income. Allowances are a form of income that kids often receive for doing work at home. Another word for income is revenue.

Point to Ponder

Think about these questions. What is the purpose and value of earning an allowance? How should the size of an allowance be determined and what type of work should be performed in order to earn an allowance? What other sources might a teenager have for earning money?

Project to Pursue

Think of several different businesses that kids could open and operate in order to generate income for themselves. Write down several possibilities and a brief description for each one. Try to be creative and resourceful in your ideas. How about a tutoring service, a pet care service, or a cookie baking/delivery service? Develop a booklet of your suggestions and distribute it to interested students who might enjoy becoming entrepreneurs.

The Aloha State _____ ICEBREAKER 4

The beautiful state of Hawaii was the fiftieth state to be admitted to the United States of America. Hawaii is actually composed of a string of islands that were formed by volcanic eruptions that left a surface of hard lava worn down over the years to form exotic black beaches. The exotic foods, beautiful beaches, warm tropical breezes, and diverse population make Hawaii a tourist destination for people from all over the world.

Point to Ponder

Plan a ten-day vacation for two to be given away as a prize by the Hawaiian Tourists Association. Include activities and recreational and cultural opportunities suitable for people of any age.

Project to Pursue

1. Taking into account air travel, hotels, ground transportation, fees for beaches, events, and food, what is your best estimate of the value of this prize?
2. If you won the prize, who would you select to go with you? Why did you choose this person?

Amazing Artifacts_____ ICEBREAKER 5

Artifacts can most simply be described as things made by people rather than things formed by nature. Scientists have found that one of the best ways to learn about the lives and cultures of people living at different periods of history is through the study of the artifacts they left behind. This study of ancient civilizations' artifacts led to archaeology as we know it today. Archaeologists have discovered treasures that are worth a great deal of money. Even more important, many of these finds have given valuable insights into the development of world history. Some excavations have even uncovered entire lost civilizations.

Point to Ponder
What influence have computers and other modern means of gathering and organizing information had on archaeology?

Project to Pursue
Make a list of six artifacts you would leave behind for scientists to use to study your society. Write a brief paragraph telling your reason for the selections.

Analyzing Advertising _____ ICEBREAKER 6

Advertising is a big business today, and it has an important influence on the spending habits of consumers. In an effort to influence the consumer to choose a specific product, "facts" about the product may be slanted in a misleading direction. Persuasive words and phrases are often used that distort or elaborate on the product's qualities and benefits to encourage impulse buying. Advertisements are often designed to describe the product in glowing and persuasive terms that are not entirely true.

Point to Ponder
What features make a newspaper or magazine ad attractive to you? Are you easily influenced?

Project to Pursue
Read the newspaper ad below to determine its accuracy. Then rewrite the ad to present only the facts.

Hurry! Hurry! This is one sale you can't afford to miss. The world's absolutely best running shoes for 50% less than retail price. BeeBop running shoes are guaranteed to last longer than any other running shoes on the market. They should last at least three years. Constructed with top quality materials and superior craftsmanship, these are absolutely the best shoes available anywhere. Come to One Stop Shoe Store at 22 Main Street before it's too late!

Animal Communication _____ ICEBREAKER 7

Although animals cannot talk as humans do, they can communicate with one another by passing on certain messages through various signs and sounds. When a mother hen makes a loud noise or crouches down, her chicks know they are in danger. When a dog lifts a paw or bares his teeth, other dogs know what is being shared. Animals also communicate with one another through smells. Most animals that live in herds depend on smell to keep together. Apes are supposed to be among the most intelligent animals, but they also talk to each other through instinctive behavior rather than learned behavior or languages as people do.

Point to Ponder

Good communication among people depends on their ability to both speak clearly and listen actively. What are some barriers that you encounter when trying to convey an important message, feeling, or idea to your teachers, parents, or friends?

Project to Pursue

Write a poem or short story using the title: "Talk to the Animals!"

Architectural Analysis _____ ICEBREAKER 8

Do you consider an architect to be an artist or a scientist? If we define architecture as the art and science of making buildings and other structures useful and beautiful, then which is more important: aesthetics or efficiency? We see the architect as a scientist because he or she must design buildings to be proportionately correct and structurally sound. He or she must also make the most efficient use of the materials and equipment available to construct buildings within particular budgets. We also see the architect as an artist because of consideration he or she gives to the use of shapes, colors, lines, and relationships making the structure attractive, comfortable, and functional. The architecture of buildings has a direct influence on the health, welfare, and outlook of the people who live and work in them. Throughout the ages, architecture has been viewed as an honorable and highly respected profession and as a great service to the advancement and enhancement of human life.

Point to Ponder

Select three buildings in your community that have very distinct architectural styles. Which of the three buildings do you rate as "the best"? Is your choice based more on attractiveness or efficiency?

Project to Pursue

Compare and contrast the features of these buildings. Use a Venn diagram to show your findings.

The Art of Acupuncture _____ ICEBREAKER 9

Acupuncture has been used in Chinese medicine for thousands of years. It involves the use of needles in the body to heal diseases and control pain. These needles vary in length from one to ten inches and are inserted at one or more of over 800 points lying along certain lines on the human body. Acupuncture is used instead of anesthesia to control pain during surgery. It is also used on patients who have chronic pain conditions such as backaches, headaches, and abdominal pain.

Point to Ponder

Think about the art and science of acupuncture. What makes sense to you about its purpose and its practice? What questions would you like to ask someone who is an acupuncturist or someone who uses acupuncture regularly?

Project to Pursue

Design both a business card for an acupuncturist and an announcement telling others about the opening of a new acupuncture clinic.

Ask a Stupid Question, _____ ICEBREAKER 10
Get a Foolish Answer

Asking good questions is both an art and a science. Many times people are unclear when they ask a question and as a result, the answer they receive is often vague, inaccurate, or impractical. Teachers try to ask students good questions so that the they can demonstrate what they know or how they think. Questions are low-level if they have one right answer and are high-level if they are open-ended with many possible answers.

Point to Ponder

Which type of questions are easiest for you to answer on a classroom quiz or test—low-level questions or high-level questions? Do you think better when there is only one possible answer to a question or when there are multiple answers to a question? Why do you think this is so?

Project to Pursue

Read each of the stupid or trite questions below and their corresponding foolish answers. Then create a few such question and answer situations of your own.

"Is that you?" "I'm not sure. I haven't looked in the mirror lately."
"Why does your room look like a tornado hit it?" "I had a brainstorm."
"Are you wearing braces?" "No, this is the latest thing in tooth jewelry."

Australia

Australia has often been referred to as the island continent because it is surrounded by water. It is the smallest continent of all and is still sparsely populated in many areas. A large percentage of the population is clustered in the cities, leaving vast territories still relatively uninhabited. Australia's chief exports include wool, wheat, and meat, while manufacturing also contributes to the economy. Many plants and animals that thrive in Australia are native to no other environment. The kangaroo and the koala are animals for which Australia is well-known.

Point to Ponder

How easy would it be for the kangaroo and/or the koala to adjust to a life in captivity? Which of the two do you think could adjust more easily? Support your answer.

Project to Pursue

Develop a plot and sequence chart for a two-volume documentary based on Australia. Outline the script, including eight to ten major topics to be featured.

The Automobile Engine

An automobile engine is the power source that drives the car. Its major source of power are the cylinders. The pistons in the cylinders work on a four-stroke cycle. It is the third stroke which is called the power stroke because a mixture of air and fuel vapor is ignited by an electric spark. The force of the explosion pushes the pistons down the cylinders. The rest of the engine captures the power and uses it to move the car.

Point to Ponder

Some people refer to their cars, complete with powerful engines, as if they were female. It is not uncommon for someone to say: "She needs some gas," or "She has to go to the shop for a grease job," or "Her engine isn't as smooth as it should be." What else can you think of besides automobiles that is often referred to as "she"?

Project to Pursue

Design an automobile of the future that is especially created for students who are learning how to drive.

Back to Basics

Many critics of American education claim that today's schools are very lax in their effort to teach the basic facts and concepts of reading, writing, and math. They argue that students of today are poorly prepared for advanced education and consequently for satisfactory performance in careers of their choice.

Point to Ponder

Is the "Back to the Basics" movement having a positive or a negative influence on today's schools? What influences, if any, is it having on the attitudes of teachers and students in your school?

Project to Pursue

Prepare a short position paper stating your opinions about using standardized achievement tests as a means of determining the extent of students' mastery of basic skills and concepts.

Basketball, Then and Now

Did you know that the game of basketball was invented by a man named James Naismith and that the first game was played at a Springfield, Massachusetts, YMCA gym in 1891? Are you surprised to learn that Mr. Naismith facilitated the game by tacking real peach baskets to the walls and making the object of the game be for a player to land the ball in the appropriate peach basket? Can you imagine the progress of the game as someone had to climb up on a ladder to remove the ball after each successful shot?

Point to Ponder

How do you think school basketball teams and the games they play have changed since 1891? Consider equipment, uniforms, playing courts, and team mobility, along with other items of your choice.

Project to Pursue

The facts about the history of basketball would provide some interesting trivia for a board game. Choose one sport from your school's intramural offering and make a list of facts that could be used as the basis for a game like Trivial Pursuit™.

Beastly Jargon _____ ICEBREAKER 15

For decades, different species of animals have been identified with certain traits of human behavior. Most of the time we apply these animal characteristics in a negative context rather than use them as a positive expression of communication. We call someone batty when we think he or she is crazy. We refer to someone as a birdbrain when he or she says or does something stupid. We label someone a jellyfish when we think he or she is a weak character, and we target someone as a leech when he or she attaches him- or herself to another without giving something back. Finally, we single someone out as a lone wolf when he or she prefers being alone to being with others.

Point to Ponder

Give a logical explanation for each of the uncomplimentary animal expressions above that is based on scientific fact about that animal's behavior or traits.

Project to Pursue

Create a comic strip depicting one of the animal personalities discussed above.

A Beautiful Shell _____ ICEBREAKER 16

Chances are you have admired an abalone shell and have agreed that it is one of the most beautiful shells in the world. The abalone is a large shellfish, found along the coasts of western North America, China, and Japan. The abalone, unlike the oyster, has only one shell. The shell's lining of mother of pearl makes it appear to be a treasure worthy of saving. And actually it is saved to be treasured through its use in buttons, cameos, ornamentation for musical instruments, and many other decorations.

Point to Ponder

The abalone is a mollusk. A sea shell is the hard covering of a sea animal belonging to the mollusk family. How many mollusk shells could you identify? How can you learn more about abalones and other mollusks?

Project to Pursue

Think of a brand-new use for the beautiful abalone shell. Describe the product and its uses and draw a sketch of it.

Beethoven's Legacy _____ ICEBREAKER 17

The work of Ludwig van Beethoven has brought joy and pleasure to music lovers around the world. It is as well loved today as in the 1800s when he made his first concert appearance in Germany at the age of eight. Beethoven wrote nine symphonies; sonatas for violin, piano, and cello; folksongs; and other songs. From the age of four, the child prodigy practiced the piano and worked diligently at his pursuit of excellence with discipline and determination.

Point to Ponder

Do you think it is harder or easier for a talented person today to commit his or her entire life to achieving excellence in his or her field than it was in the 1800s?

Project to Pursue

Compare and contrast the contribution to future generations made by a master artist or musician to that of an equally dedicated and productive scientist.

The Beginnings of Kissing _____ ICEBREAKER 18

Most likely, kissing started as an expression of homage and respect in other parts of the world. For example, many African tribes required that the natives kiss the ground that the chief walked on, and the early Romans kissed a person's mouth or eyes as a form of dignified greeting. The first country where the kiss became a ritual of affection and courtship was France. It then spread rapidly all over Europe. Today the kiss is truly a sign of love as it has become an important part of the wedding ceremony.

Point to Ponder

Describe the many ways that people in government, politics, or business pay homage and show respect to one another. Does the kiss ever play a role in these situations?

Project to Pursue

What are some other forms of greeting? Compare and contrast greetings in the United States and Canada to greetings in other countries. What do these greetings tell us about other cultures?

Belated Appreciation ICEBREAKER **19**

Vincent van Gogh's paintings are among the most prized by art collectors today. It is a pity that in his own lifetime the works of this Dutch painter, who early on moved to France to work, were not popular at all. His use of strong colors and textures was too bold for the taste of art lovers of the late 1800s. His work did not even afford him an income for the barest necessities. He had difficulty making friends, depended on his brother for support, and took his own life at the very time he was painting some of the works that today sell for millions of dollars.

Point to Ponder

1. Do you think the average citizen of your age appreciates the arts more or less than citizens of your parents' age? Support your answer with three examples.
2. Does your school provide adequate education in art appreciation? If not, what could be done to remedy the situation?

Project to Pursue

Compare and contrast the economic opportunities available to artists living today with those of the nineteenth century. Make a list of ways aspiring artists today might supplement their incomes and/or gain support for their works.

Ben Franklin ICEBREAKER **20**

Most of Benjamin Franklin's early teachers must have been surprised to learn of his later fame as one of America's important inventors and philosophers. The self-taught student excelled in many ways. He was a printer, author, publisher, inventor, scientist, businessman, and statesman. Of all his accomplishments, he is probably best remembered for his publication of *Poor Richard's Almanac*. Many of the sayings in this collection were based on Ben Franklin's strong commitment to thrifty habits, good character, and personal integrity.

Point to Ponder

Is it harder or easier for truly gifted and multitalented people in today's highly mobile and complex society to develop and use their talents and abilities than it was one hundred years ago? What influence does technology have on the issue?

Project to Pursue

Begin a book of quotes appropriate for promoting good character and personal integrity. Try to include at least six to ten quotes, each with an easily discernible message.

Beware of the Beetles _____ ICEBREAKER **21**

The common name *beetle* identifies one of the largest and most diverse groups of insects. Some of the better known beetles are the June bug, boll weevil, potato bug, and firefly. Not so well known are the museum beetles which live in glass cases and chew up the case's contents, the carpet beetle that thrives on carpets, and blind beetles found in underground coves where they live in total darkness. Some beetles actually live their whole lives in a nest of ants who feed and pamper them as if they were pets.

Point to Ponder

Would you view the beetle more as predator or prey?

Project to Pursue

Beetles form one of the most harmful of all groups of insects. They destroy crops, foodstuffs, trees, clothing, and many more consumer products. Ladybugs are among the few exceptions, as they actually help farmers by eating harmful insects. Write an ode in praise of the ladybug.

A Bird to Admire _____ ICEBREAKER **22**

The picture that is apt to come to mind when the word *stork* is mentioned is that of a long-legged, strong-winged bird carrying a baby in a diaper in its mouth. The stork has become a legend of folklore and a symbol of a baby's arrival. This legend probably began when people observed the loving care the stork exhibits for its own young. A stork couple's faithfulness to each other also serves as a model for married happiness. Storks build nests on roofs and chimneys close to homes inhabited by human beings. They seek food such as eels, frogs, toads, and other small animals in marshes and swamps. In many parts of the world the stork is a much respected and highly protected bird.

Point to Ponder

What lessons can be learned by observing and learning more about the habits of birds such as the stork? Why is it important to protect and study them?

Project to Pursue

Create a brand-new legend about a stork who became a hero through some act of bravery involving a small child.

The Black Death _____ ICEBREAKER 23

The black death was actually an outbreak of bubonic plague which ravaged Asia and Europe between 1334 and 1351. It was carried by fleas that lived on rats inhabiting ships and overland trading caravans traveling westward. The bubonic plague was named after the buboes, or swellings, that appeared on the bodies of its victims. About one person in three died from the disease during this time. Bodies were carried away for burial by designated corpse-collectors.

Point to Ponder

Determine what would be the worst thing about being a corpse-collector during the age of the bubonic plague. Decide on something that might be good about the situation.

Project to Pursue

Research to discover what nursery rhymes developed in this time period. Which ones refer to the plague itself? Compare and contrast the life of a child who lived during the time of the plague to the life of a child today.

Body Numbers _____ ICEBREAKER 24

Numbers can tell us a lot about how the body functions. Some number facts that people find interesting are these:
1. Your body contains 8 pints of blood.
2. Your body is 70% water.
3. The small intestines are 20 feet long and the large intestines are 5 feet long.
4. An eyelash lives about 150 days before it falls out.
5. Your heart beats about 100,000 times a day.
6. Your brain sends messages at the rate of 240 mph.
7. You have about 120,000 hairs on your head.
8. About 400 gallons of blood flow through your kidneys in one day.

Point to Ponder

Decide on which of the number facts above is most surprising to you and why. How could you use these number facts to help you maintain a healthy body?

Project to Pursue

Write a short thank you note to your kidneys, a want ad for a heart, or an apology to your intestines for overeating.

Body Snatchers _____ ICEBREAKER 25

During the 1700s in Britain, one popular trade was body snatching, because medical schools needed corpses that could be used in the training of future doctors. Medical students would dissect the corpses to learn more about the human body structure. The majority of body snatchers worked at night digging bodies from graveyards where the dead had just been buried.

Point to Ponder

Today doctors and scientists also use animals in research as they try to discover new ways to cure human diseases. Animal rights advocates claim this practice is immoral and inhumane and should be prohibited. Do you think the potential good that such research can provide humans (for example, a cure for cancer or AIDS) outweighs the suffering of the animals?

Project to Pursue

Write and act out a short skit enacting a pair of body snatchers at work in a local cemetery.

Bone Basics _____ ICEBREAKER 26

The main job of bones in the body is to give shape to the frame. Joints in the skeletal system are there to allow the bones to move in different directions. The ligaments are bands of tough tissue that hold the joints together. They are strong and flexible. The main job of the muscles is to make involuntary and voluntary body movement possible while the tendons hold the muscles to the bones.

Point to Ponder

Think about how your skeletal system would have to be different if human beings had a different habitat, such as spending most of their time in water, in trees, or in outer space.

Project to Pursue

If joints, ligaments, muscles, and tendons could talk, describe a conversation they might have with each other.

Books to Cherish
————————————— ICEBREAKER **27**

Books are the quietest and most constant of friends; they are the most accessible and wisest of counselors, and the most patient of teachers.
— Charles W. Eliot

Point to Ponder

What books would you choose to be your "constant companions" if your list of books to own had to be limited to three?

Project to Pursue

Think about the above quote and create a sketch for a poster, complete with illustrations, attractive graphics, or other elements to be used for a public awareness campaign to promote reading for your school or community. Design the poster so that it can be extended to several forms of media, i.e., television, newspapers, magazines, etc. Plan the entire campaign, including fund-raising efforts.

Brain Food
————————————————— ICEBREAKER **28**

You've heard people talk about breakfast as "the most important meal of the day" and extol its virtues as the one meal winners can't afford to skip. Yet, many research studies continue to relay findings to indicate that breakfast may be "the meal everyone talks about" but "few do little right about." A sugary doughnut, a bun on the run, or even nothing at all seems to be the breakfast of choice for too many people in today's fast-paced society. Nutritionists continue to issue warnings about the brain's susceptibility to short-term variations in nutrients and the body's need for energy to begin the daily level of both mental and physical activity. The term *breakfast* really means what it says. With the first food of the day, the night's "fast" is broken. Carbohydrates, supplying glucose which has been called "food for the brain," are an ideal breakfast choice. Fortunately they are plentifully supplied by convenience foods, including breads and cereals. So you can breakfast in a healthy way, even on the run.

Point to Ponder

Do you think health education in today's schools is being given proper emphasis? What suggestions would you make for improvement?

Project to Pursue

Make a breakfast menu that includes all of the breakfast foods you like most. Make another menu high in carbohydrates and low in fats and sugars. Compare the two. Review your breakfasts for the past week and determine how well you have been "feeding your brain" for the day ahead.

Bridging the Gap ICEBREAKER 29

Since the days when the only bridges across waterways or ravines were fallen logs, natural rock formations, or tangled vines and matted undergrowth, human beings have sought and found increasingly more efficient methods of "bridging." Bridge building as we know it today has advanced from simple timber bridges; the first pier bridge, with a pier at intervals to keep the bridge from sagging; truss bridges where the trusses are arranged so that each truss shares part of the weight; the arch bridges of Rome with the keystone at the tip of the arch relaying the pressure from stone to stone so it is distributed throughout the arch; more modern suspension bridges which rely on cables fastened to high towers on each bank; to present-day bridges, whose engineers take from all of these and other principles to design and construct the safest and most efficient bridges possible. Visionary efforts of people who studied and perfected the many types of bridges in operation throughout the world cannot be overlooked as one of humanity's greatest contributions to present-day communication, transportation, and economic stability.

Point to Ponder

Identify the location and type of bridges serving your community. How much do you know about their history?

Project to Pursue

Develop an outline for a radio or TV documentary script to inform the public about the importance of bridges in our present-day society. What are the major concepts that you wish to convey?

Bring on the Beans ICEBREAKER 30

Beans are taken for granted as a diet staple of both rich and poor around the world. In times past, the lovely bean, which is actually a member of the pea family, was looked upon as a subsistence food of country peasants and the urban poor. In more recent years, however, nutritionists have extolled its nutritional value and culinary artists have created exotic dishes to present the inexpensive bean in a whole new light. Bean dishes are now featured prominently in upscale restaurants, in gourmet magazines, and in food markets as diverse as health food stores, ethnic shops, and specialty food boutiques. Dry beans are especially valuable as a commercially marketed product. Other uses include the green fodder fed to cattle and numerous raw materials used in manufacturing consumer goods.

Point to Ponder

Think of a brand-new use for beans or the bean plant that is not a food source.

Project to Pursue

Create a new recipe with beans as the main ingredient that you would serve to a visiting dignitary from another country as representative of a traditional dish from the region in which you live.

Buffalo Bill _____

Have you heard the story of "Buffalo Bill and the Wild West Show"? The amazing thing about this story is that William Cody's stage name of "Buffalo Bill" is as well-known today as one of the all-time great American showmen as it was during the time he originated his traveling show, when the United States was still a struggling new country. With his touring company, which included bears, buffalo, horses, tepees, covered wagons, Indians, cowboys, and many other live attractions, he traveled extensively throughout the United States and Europe. In England, his show played for the Queen. Buffalo Bill's earlier life as a buffalo hunter, stage coach driver, and soldier had prepared him well for the life of adventure and excitement he encountered with his great traveling extravaganza.

Point to Ponder

Do you think "Buffalo Bill's Wild West Show" would be as exciting to people today as it was when he presented it? Why or why not?

Project to Pursue

Predict how you think William Cody would choose to present his Wild West Show if he were alive today. Would it be through TV, a Hollywood film, performances in a great hall, or as before, a touring show traveling around the world? Develop the plan for a brochure or handbill advertising the show as you envision it.

The Busy Beaver _____

The beaver is best known for its industriousness and for its habits of gnawing and cutting down trees to build dams. These habits are extremely useful for this hard-working animal since its habitat is lakes and streams in wooded areas. The beaver is a rodent, as are rats, mice, rabbits, and squirrels. Unlike its other family members, however, the beaver is a useful animal and causes little harm. Beavers are now protected from human predators, who killed so many of them for their fur that they nearly became extinct.

Point to Ponder

How does the slogan "busy as a beaver" apply to today's average worker in the work place? How does it apply to the top-ranking elected officials of your nation?·

Project to Pursue

Design a sketch and a slogan for a poster urging people to reject products made from the skins of fur-bearing animals.

Calamity Jane _____ ICEBREAKER 33

Everyone knows about the male heroes of the Wild West, but few know much about the female heroes, such as Calamity Jane. It has been said that women living in the Wild West had to be tough and none came tougher than Calamity Jane who could outride and outshoot most men in the frontier towns. She was born in Deadwood, South Dakota, and toured with Wild West shows often dressed in men's clothing and demonstrating her skill with a rifle.

Point to Ponder

Think about why some girls are called tomboys and whether this is a compliment or a criticism.

Project to Pursue

People like to gossip about individuals who act or behave in nontraditional ways. Sometimes what they say is true and sometimes what they say is merely their own opinion. Fill a series of conversation balloons with gossip statements that neighbors, friends, enemies, and acquaintances might be saying about Calamity Jane in the days of the Wild West.

Calendar Countdown _____ ICEBREAKER 34

The calendar that we take for granted today is based on work done by ancient Babylonian scientists. For long periods of time they kept careful records of their star studies which they used to develop the earliest calendars. The Romans, however, have been given credit for providing the basis of the calendar year based on 365 ¼ days in a solar year, with one extra day added every fourth year. The word *calendar* is derived from the latin word *kalendra* which means the first of the month. The concept of the calendar year made of twelve months has been in existence since before the time of Julius Caesar. Calendars used today have changed drastically since that time to better meet the needs of our fast-paced, time-sensitive society and are manufactured and sold in more different forms and with wider ranging shapes, sizes, and themes each year.

Point to Ponder

Which group—teenagers, the middle aged, or senior citizens—do you think would acclimate more quickly to the change from a twelve- to a thirteen-month calendar?

Project to Pursue

Redesign the traditional twelve-month calendar to include a thirteenth month. Account for the number of days in each of the thirteen months by taking days from the existing twelve months. Place the new month where you think it best fits. Use the new calendar to plan a new school year for your school. Include which months school would be open and school holidays to total 180 days.

The California Gold Rush _____

The gold rush was a colorful time in American history. It started at the end of 1848 when a carpenter by the name of James Wilson Marshall found nuggets of gold beside the American River, near Coloma, California, while building a sawmill. The news spread quickly and hordes of gold-hungry prospectors came to California from all over the world. Sixty shiploads of people sailed from the eastern U.S. around Cape Horn in 1849 and were known as the 49ers.

Point to Ponder

Imagine what it would be like to leave your home and family to travel a long distance in hopes of finding gold in California. What things would motivate individuals to take this action and what risks or rewards were they likely to encounter?

Project to Pursue

Design a mini-catalog for prospectors getting ready to move to California in search of gold nuggets. Be sure to include pictures and descriptions of items they would need, complete with prices and special offerings.

Capital City Charm _____

Washington, D.C., replaced Philadelphia as the capital city of the United States of America in 1800. It is the only American city that is not a part of a state. Government of the people, by the people, and for the people of the United States is Washington's primary business. The other businesses located in the District of Columbia are there chiefly to support and provide goods and services for the people whose business it is to run the government. Embassies from around the world add to the population and help to make it very diverse. Beautiful green space, wide boulevards, white marble buildings, and memorial monuments add additional color and aesthetic quality to the city's already memorable appeal.

Point to Ponder

If your class were to take a field trip to Washington, what specific educational and social goals could be achieved? How would the money for the trip be raised? How long would the total trip take and what kind of transportation would be utilized?

Project to Pursue

Write a paragraph explaining how you would handle these issues.

Catching Up on the Catch _____ ICEBREAKER 37

Alaska, the forty-ninth state admitted to the United States of America, is known worldwide as one of the world's foremost fishing sites. Shrimp, crab, halibut, herring, seals, sea lions, walruses, and whales are just some of the important "catches" taken from Alaskan waters. Fishing is one of the main industries making a valuable contribution to the state's economy. Just as hunting and lumbering resources need protection from abusive overuse, so do Alaska's waterways.

Point to Ponder

Is there a natural resource in your own state that is endangered because of commercial demand? If so, what steps need to be taken for its protection?

Project to Pursue

Pretend that you are a member of the United States Congress representing the people of Alaska. Draft a plan of action you would use to address the need for conservation and wise use of Alaska's marine resources.

Chemistry Checkup _____ ICEBREAKER 38

Chemists are scientists who devote their professional lives to studying the characteristics of matter and the manner in which different kinds of matter behave and/or react to widely varying conditions. Matter is anything that takes up space. It may be as simple as a tiny pebble or a rain drop, or as complex as a flock of wild geese or an uncut diamond. Matter comes in three states known as solids, liquids, and gasses. A liquid has mass and volume but takes the shape of its container. A gas has mass but has no specific shape and expands to fill its container. A solid has a definite shape.

Point to Ponder

Can you explain how H_2O can take the form of a solid, liquid, and a gas?

Project to Pursue

Prepare an outline for interviewing a chemist visiting your classroom as a resource speaker. Include questions you would like to ask about professional preparation, job demands, and scientific information related to the study of matter.

Chocoholics

The Aztecs are credited with being the first chocoholics because their favorite kind of drink was a cold cocoa. It was made from the beans of the cacao tree and flavored with vanilla and spices. It is said that the Emperor Montezuma was addicted to this beverage and consumed 50 jars a day himself, while the average consumption of his household was 2000 jars a day.

Point to Ponder

Determine what criteria one would use to identify and diagnose a "chocoholic." Think of some causes of this imaginary disease and some possible ways to cure it.

Project to Pursue

Draw a picture of a scene that shows what would happen on "the day it rained chocolate kisses and chocolate caramels."

The Cold War

After World War II, there have been many local wars between small countries. The great powers of the former Soviet Union, the United States, and Great Britain have also experienced times of great tension, but instead of armed conflicts and battles, these have resulted in something called the "cold wars." This simply means that the great powers closed their economic markets and refused to sell their products to each other. This very often produced great economic hardships as well as hard times and hard feelings.

Point to Ponder

Think about what it means when someone receives "the cold shoulder" from a group of friends, neighbors, or family members. Determine how this might relate to the notion of "cold wars" between countries or nations.

Project to Pursue

Create an editorial cartoon that depicts the concept of a "cold war" between one or more countries or the "cold shoulder" between one or more political figures.

Common Childhood Conditions ____ ICEBREAKER 41

Kids often encounter a variety of common childhood illnesses and conditions caused by germs. Much school is missed because of these afflictions and much anguish is experienced because of these nuisance ailments. Some of these include: 1) acne, which is caused by bacteria and oil in the skin clogging pores which then become inflamed; 2) athlete's foot, which is caused by a fungus that itches and irritates the skin between the toes; 3) colds, which are caused by viruses in the respiratory tract; and 4) warts, which are caused by a virus in the skin cells which causes rapid growth of the skin's outer layer.

Point to Ponder

Rank each of these common childhood conditions in terms of their impact on you as a kid. Which one is the worst thing to have, and which one is the least cause for concern, and where do the others fall in between?

Project to Pursue

Make up a five-way conversation between each of these conditions using bubbles for recording various statements. What would they be saying to one another?

Creatures of the Night _____ ICEBREAKER 42

When people refer to a person as a "wise old owl" they are probably using the term to imply that the person is solemn looking and seems very attentive. If a person is referred to as a "night owl," he or she probably stays up until the wee hours of the morning. If someone is referred to as a "guardian owl," this person may very well be a gardener who strives to rid gardens of rats, mice, and other rodents that devour plants by moonlight. Even though there are more than five hundred known species of owls these descriptions for the most part fit very well. One commonly held belief about owls, however, is untrue. Owls have often been believed to be blind in the daylight and capable of seeing only at night. This misconception may have arisen because many species of owls do prefer to eat at night because it is easier for them to swoop down and capture their rodent prey as they scurry around in the dark. Although the vision of an owl may be somewhat limited at night, hearing becomes more keen than in the day because there are fewer distractions.

Point to Ponder

Can an owl truly turn its head 360 degrees? If not, how far can it turn?

Project to pursue

Sketch a portrait of a person (real or imaginary) you would label as a "wise old owl." Write a brief character sketch of the person.

Customs and Cultures _____ ICEBREAKER 43

Every culture has its own set of traditions, traits, and timelines. These customs are important for people to respect and understand as our world is getting so much smaller and so much more interdependent in part because of rapid economic growth and expanding telecommunications. Review some of these interesting customs and think about how they would be important to know if you were to visit that country.
- In India, women wear rings through their noses to show they are married.
- In New Zealand, gum chewing in public is thought to be impolite.
- In Taiwan, belching and burping after a meal is considered to be a compliment to the cook.
- In the Philippines, it is polite to be late to social affairs.
- In South Korea, pushing and shoving in stores and streets is normal and acceptable behavior.

Point to Ponder

Think of some rituals and customs practiced by Americans that might seem strange to people visiting the United States from other countries or cultures.

Project to Pursue

Pretend you are going to make a time capsule representing the American way of life during the 1990s. Make a list of ten items that you would place in the time capsule and give reasons for each one.

Decode the Message _____ ICEBREAKER 44

Louis Braille invented the braille alphabet in 1824. In the years since, this special code made up of small raised dots that can be read by touch has changed the lives of many blind persons. The Morse code, developed by Samuel Morse as an aid to transmitting messages by telegraph in the United States and Canada in 1837, was another code of importance in the history of communication. Actually, the English language can be thought of as a spoken and written code. When we read the English language, we are decoding the message someone has written. When we write the English language we are encoding a message for someone else to decode.

Point to Ponder

A code can be developed when a meaning is established that each person using the code understands. The elements of the code are symbols that represent concepts to others. Think of other kinds of symbols that you see everyday (ex. colors). Why are symbols so important to us?

Project to Pursue

Develop a brand new code of your own using alphabetical order of letters, numerical order, words, signs, or pictures. Use your code to write a message to a friend. Give the friend your coding system and the message to decode. Based on the ease of decoding, determine the effectiveness of your code.

Digging Digits _____ ICEBREAKER **45**

A digit is a single number. In the decimal system of counting, the digits are zero (0) through nine (9). This system is called a base ten numbering system. Can you guess why? Digits can be used to write even larger numbers. The number 10,675 has five digits which are 1, 0, 6, 7, and 5. In the binary system, there are only two digits, 0 and 1. Another name for a digit is a numeral.

Point to Ponder

Explain in your own words how to add the following numbers: 88, .03, and 5.7.

Project to Pursue

Create a comic strip character using a digit from 0 to 9 as the basis for your drawing. Name your character and design a scenario showing him or her in action.

D Is for Dictionary and Definitions _ ICEBREAKER **46**

The dictionary is an invaluable tool for school, home, and work. Dictionaries provide the user with many different types of information. In most dictionaries, a person can find not only the correct spelling, pronunciation, and definitions for a given word, but also its origins, parts of speech, and various spellings or variations of the word. Dictionaries come in many shapes and sizes with versions written for young children and large print or braille versions for people with vision problems.

Point to Ponder

Discuss how a dictionary and a thesaurus are alike and how they are different. Determine when one is more useful to a reader or a writer than another.

Project to Pursue

Research to learn about Noah Webster. Write a brief paragraph about his life. What was different about his dictionary?

Don't Be a Lame Brain _____ ICEBREAKER 47

Did you know that your brain is divided into two halves? The left half of your brain learns facts and figures, and the right half of your brain learns how to think and write creatively. People who have a left brain tendency are most often very logical, rational, organized, and structured. People who have a right brain tendency are most often very flexible, intuitive, spontaneous, and impulsive. Most of the curriculum in school teaches left brain thinking so it is important to nurture the right half of the brain when you can.

Point to Ponder

Do you think you are more of a left brain thinker or a right brain thinker? Give reasons for your answer.

Project to Pursue

Practice this right brain exercise: If you were a telephone, what would you talk about? Without telling your friend what you are, pick an object like a radio or a refrigerator. Instruct your friend to start a conversation by asking about your day, and you respond as the object. How many questions does your friend have to ask before he or she can guess what you are? Reverse roles and try this activity again using different objects.

Don't Be Fooled by a Rattlesnake ___ ICEBREAKER 48

Rattlesnakes don't shake their rattles to warn people to stay away. In fact, 95% of the time they give no advanced notice that they are about to strike. Rattlesnakes tend to vibrate their tails rapidly because they are frightened. Poisonous snakes both strike and bite their enemies. The cobra is a more dangerous snake than the rattlesnake because it is more aggressive and because its venom is more deadly. Rattlesnakes have longer fangs than cobras, but the cobra hangs on to and chews its prey for a longer period of time.

Point to Ponder

Even though most snakes people encounter in their local environment are harmless, people are deathly afraid of snakes. Explain why you think this is true and what a person can do to overcome this fear.

Project to Pursue

Snakes can shed their skins. Draw a cartoon to show what life would be like if people could shed their skins in certain situations.

Don't Be Speechless _____ ICEBREAKER 49

How often have you admired or envied someone in your class who could present information, speeches, or demonstrations with ease and confidence? People who speak and present well are not often naturally talented speakers, but rather have had opportunities to learn and practice public speaking skills. In giving a speech, presenters:
- use quotations, anecdotes, statistics, or analogies in their speech development;
- use notes or cue words to avoid looking uncomfortable and/or over-rehearsed;
- use visual aids or images to enhance the information which they are presenting;
- use strategies to keep their listeners from getting bored;
- use good voice inflections and body language gestures.

Point to Ponder

Researchers have found that "giving a speech" is one of the most feared and dreaded activities required of both kids and adults. Think about a time when you were asked to do an oral report, presentation, demonstration, or speech and it caused you a great deal of anxiety. How did you fare?

Project to Pursue

Compile a list of topics for impromptu speeches. Use these with a group of friends to practice one or more of the speech skills listed above.

Dreams to Die For _____ ICEBREAKER 50

Martin Luther King, Jr., is recognized as the leader of the civil rights movement in the United States. He ran numerous voter registration campaigns for African Americans and used nonviolent disobedience to fight for desegregation. In 1963, he organized the March on Washington where he inspired many with his "I Have a Dream" speech. He began to campaign against economic as well as racial discrimination, and he was planning a multiracial poverty march on Washington to demand the funding of an "Economic Bill of Rights" when he was assassinated in Memphis, TN, on April 4, 1968. He gave his life for his dream of racial equality.

Point to Ponder

Think of three or four other well-known figures from history who have had dreams that have controlled the destiny of their lives. Determine the effects of these dreams on future generations.

Project to Pursue

Write a brief paragraph describing a "dream for the future" of your own. Sketch an illustration for your dream.

Drumming It Up _____

Drums are popular instruments in bands and orchestras. The kind of sound a drum makes depends on how you hit it and the size of the drum. A drumstick gives a harsh crack, while a mallet or a pair of hands give a plump sound. A drum is made from a piece of skin which is stretched over the frame of the drum. The bigger the skin, the deeper and louder the sound. When the drum is hit, the skin vibrates and makes a sound. It also makes the frame and the air inside the frame to vibrate and these sounds then mix with the sound of the skin.

Point to Ponder

A common expression that is used in conversation is: "Oh, please don't drum all that stuff up again." How do you think this relates to the drum as an instrument?

Project to Pursue

Using a pair of pencils, practice playing a drum on the top of a glass bottle, a tin can, a wooden table, a cardboard box, and a plastic dish. Create a series of rhythmic pieces to play for your friends.

Examining Television Violence_____

Recently, a year-long study was completed on violence in television entertainment. The results of this study were staggering:
1. Perpetrators of violent acts on TV go unpunished 73% of the time. That could mean "viewers are more likely to learn the lesson that violence is successful," researchers concluded.
2. Researchers found that 47% of all violent interactions show no harm to victims and 58% depict no pain. Longer-term consequences such as financial or emotional harm were shown only 16% of the time.
3. Some 25% of violent incidents on TV involve the use of handguns.
4. Few programs containing violence (4%) emphasize nonviolent alternatives in solving problems.

Point to Ponder

Discuss what appeal violent shows on television have for the average child, teenager, and adult. Determine what might be done about it.

Project to Pursue

Think about television shows that you watch on a weekly basis and write down the names of those shows that seem to reflect the factual information given above. Design a crossword puzzle using these show titles. Vary your clues for each show and make them challenging. Be sure to spell the show titles correctly.

An Exciting City

New York City has been labeled by many world travelers as the most exciting city in the world. When looking at all that this bustling, history-rich city has to offer it is easy to understand this label. It is visited by teenagers and senior citizens alike as often today as it was a hundred years ago. It is host to the United Nations and home of the New York Stock Exchange, giant banks, and worldwide conglomerate business headquarters. It supports a multitude of enrichment opportunities such as Central Park, museums and galleries, theater, and music and dance performances galore. Trade, commerce, and shopping beyond the wildest imagination and the rich cultural diversity of its population help to earn New York its claim to fame. The Statue of Liberty, gracing the harbor with its torch held high to welcome arrivals from around the world, provides a symbolic touchstone for New York City's impressive skyline. What an exciting city!

Point to Ponder

If you had only one day to spend in New York City, which of its many attractions would you choose to visit? If your parents or other adults in your family were accompanying you, would they agree with your choice? If not, what kind of compromise would be possible?

Project to Pursue

Make a list of twenty adjectives that could be used to describe some aspect of New York City. Use at least half of the adjectives in a summary paragraph for a travel brochure to be distributed to would-be visitors from a country other than the United States.

Eyes of Interest

A snake has no movable eyelids. Snakes see through windows protected by rough plates that are shed with their skin.

The hippopotamus has eyes on the tip of its head which enable it to look out for danger.

Birds have a third eyelid.

Fish have lidless eyes which are protected by the water in which they live.

Point to Ponder

Why is it important for students to learn as much as they can about animal characteristics and habits?

Project to Pursue

Use a Venn diagram to compare and contrast the use of contact lenses and eyeglasses to correct vision problems. Consider availability, convenience, costs, appearance, and long-range effectiveness.

Fables to Capture your Fancy

Aesop's fables are short stories about animals that illustrate the faults and virtues of human beings. It is believed that many of these stories were brought to Greece from the east more than two thousand years ago. A slave in Greece named Aesop has been given credit for making them popular. The first collection of the fables took place more than two hundred years after Aesop's death. Aesop was also given credit for similar stories that were later added to the collection. And so, Aesop's fables have lived throughout the ages to delight storytellers, listeners, and readers with their straightforward plots, animal characters, and "lessons to be learned."

Point to Ponder

There must be something very special about Aesop's fables to have caused them to remain popular for more than two thousand years. What do you think it is?

Project to Pursue

The fable of the grasshopper who lazed away the summer while the industrious ant was busily storing food for the winter is one of the most famous of Aesop's fables. The ant's answer to the grasshoppers request for food ("since you sang all summer, you can dance all winter") has been used many times to demonstrate the value of perseverance and foresight. Create another fable using different animal characters to convey the same lesson.

Factually Speaking

Good readers know that it is important to learn to distinguish fact from opinion. Sometimes it is hard for even the most avid readers to tell the difference. A skillful writer with a mastery of word usage may combine a little bit of information with a lot of imagination and a dash of his or her own opinion to present a biased and less than factual portrayal of a subject. The critical reader learns to question the source of written material and the authority of the author in order to determine if the information is one-hundred-percent factual.

Point to Ponder

Think of other statements based on opinion that are commonly accepted by many people. Question the possible consequences of accepting each of these statements as factual.

Project to Pursue

Select one of the statements below and write a paragraph to disprove it. Tell why the statement is not one-hundred-percent factual, how it may have started as an opinion and became accepted as a fact, and why it is important to question and/or prove the inaccuracy of the statement.
1. Eskimos live in igloos.
2. Teenagers today are more selfish than they were fifty years ago.
3. Pet owners are kind people.

Fasting Means Little or No Food _____ ICEBREAKER 57

When one fasts, one does not eat at all or does not eat special foods for a predetermined period of time. Most of the time people fast for religious purposes, although some people choose to fast for political or health reasons as well. Muslims fast from dawn to sunset during the holy month of Ramadan so that their sins will be forgiven. Jews fast on the holy day of Yom Kippur to atone for their wrongdoings. Christians fast during Lent, forty days that commemorate the forty days Jesus fasted in the desert.

Point to Ponder

Think about your own family and culture. Is there a time of the year when it might be a good idea for you to fast? If so, when would it be and what foods would you give up?

Project to Pursue

The day before Lent begins is known as Mardi Gras, or Fat Tuesday. Many people throw big parties, and several cities, especially New Orleans, have parades and public celebrations to indulge themselves before their period of self-deprivation. Design your own costume or mask to wear to a Mardi Gras celebration.

The Father of Geometry _____ ICEBREAKER 58

Geometry is an important branch of mathematics that deals with sizes and shapes of various plane and solid figures. Euclid, a Greek philosopher born in 330 B.C., wrote the first book on the topic and is known as the "father of geometry." This book, entitled *Elements*, contains geometric proofs and theories including the famous one known as the Pythagorean theorem. A proof explains why a theory is correct, and Euclid's proofs are so clever they are still being used today.

Point to Ponder

Brainstorm as many reasons as you can think of for studying geometry in school. Consider how geometry is used in art, architecture, nature, road/bridge construction, and fashion.

Project to Pursue

Create a book jacket for a new middle school textbook in geometry. Be sure to write something about the book on one of the inside flaps and something about the author on the other inside flap.

The First Book _____ ICEBREAKER 59

Johannes Gutenberg, a German craftsman, printed the first book, a Bible, around the middle of the fifteenth century. He invented a system with movable type, which was a kind of stamp, called a punch, on which a letter of the alphabet was engraved. Punches could then be arranged to form a word. Before Gutenberg, books were handwritten and illustrated with miniature paintings. Gutenberg's system made it possible to reproduce texts that until then had always been written by hand. Before his invention, there were only a few copies of each book.

Point to Ponder

Many inventions have revolutionized the world, but none as remarkably as Gutenberg's printing press. Think of as many arguments as you can to support the idea that Gutenberg's "movable type" is the most important invention ever created over time.

Project to Pursue

Take a page from a favorite novel, short story, or textbook and copy the entire page by hand using manuscript printing, not cursive writing. Try to illustrate some of the ideas with miniature drawings or paintings. Keep track of the time it takes you to complete this tedious task.

A Flight with No Return _____ ICEBREAKER 60

Amelia Earhart was born in 1898 at a time when women were not expected to be driving trains, sailing ships, or flying airplanes. During World War I, while she was serving as a nurse's aid at a military hospital, Amelia became fascinated with airplanes. It was at that point that she determined to become a pilot. After flying solo across the Atlantic Ocean in 1932, she planned a flight around the world to complete a route that had never been flown before. In 1937, she and her navigator set off on this 27,000 mile flight never to return. With only 7,000 miles left to go, they lost radio contact and have never been heard from since.

Point to Ponder

Would Amelia Earhart's name be so well-known today if her flight had ended successfully?

Project to Pursue

In your own words describe the influence you think Amelia Earhart's courage and determination had on women of her time.

Flowcharts Are In! _____ ICEBREAKER 61

Computers and technology have made flowcharts an important tool for business and industry in today's society. A flowchart is a diagram that shows the steps in solving a problem or in accomplishing a task. The steps must be arranged in a specific order or sequence so that each step leads logically to the next one. Flowcharts make good visual aids when there is a need to help make complex problems easier to analyze.

Point to Ponder

People solve problems or complete tasks in many different ways. Some are said to be auditory learners who prefer to hear about solutions or steps for accomplishing a task. Others are said to be visual learners who prefer diagrams and drawings that represent solutions and tasks. Still others are kinesthetic or tactile learners who prefer constructing their own flowcharts to solve problems or complete a task. How do you learn best?

Project to Pursue

Construct a simple diagram or flowchart to show others how to do something. Can you visually demonstrate how to write a book report, make a batch of fudge, or ask for a raise in your allowance?

Flowers that Never Wilt _____ ICEBREAKER 62

An anonymous philosopher said, "Flowers to nourish the soul are as important to human growth and development as is bread to nourish the body."
Claude Monet was a French artist who painted beautiful flowers, landscapes, and pleasant scenes reminiscent of nature's wonders. Monet lived from 1840 to 1926 and is particularly well-known for his use of pastel watercolors and for paintings inspired by his lovely gardens at Givenchy in the south of France. His paintings shown today are highly prized by art collectors and collections of his works are exhibited at some of the finest galleries and museums in the world. Needless to say, the work of this great artist has brought joy, happiness, and appreciation for art and nature to many people throughout the world.

Point to Ponder

1. Agree or disagree with the philosopher's statement above. Support your position with an application to your own life.
2. Many of Monet's paintings have been adapted and reproduced on commercially marketed products such as bags, scarves, boxes, book covers, and mugs. Do you think this is a good use of the work of master artists? Give five reasons for your answer.

Project to Pursue

List as many places as you can where people in your own community can go to enjoy and celebrate some form of the arts. Make a check mark beside the ones you have visited.

Frankenstein's Monster _____ ICEBREAKER 63

Many people don't know that the story of the scientist Frankenstein and the monster he created was actually written by a woman, Mary Shelley. It was published in 1818. Mary fell in love with the poet Percy Bysshe Shelley and married him after his wife died in 1816. Mary spent much of her life writing herself and editing her husband's work. Frankenstein is her most famous publication. It is a story of how the monster made by Frankenstein saw so much cruelty and evil in the world that he turned against it.

Point to Ponder

Explain why you think so many kids are fascinated by monsters and monster stories or movies. What different forms do monsters take in literature and in fantasy?

Project to Pursue

Make a list of the ten scariest words you can think of and then use them to write a short monster story of your own.

From Arctic Wolf to Zebra _____ ICEBREAKER 64

The animal kingdom is composed of an awe-inspiring collection of many wondrous and splendid creatures from insects so small they are barely visible to the human eye to the blue whale, whose height, weight, and length are enormous. An amazing thing that animals have in common is their adaptability to their own habitat and their ability to coexist with other living things within their environment. For example, the arctic wolf, who lives in the tundra of Arctic North America and Greenland, is a very large and bold animal who during the long winter months adapts to its harsh environment by preying upon larger animals such as the musk ox. Another amazing thing is the uniqueness of each animal; each one is different and special in its own way. The zebra, which roams wild in Africa living for the most part in small bands led by a stallion, is differentiated from all other members of the genus *Equus* by its bold colors and zigzag-striped body.

Point to Ponder

Consider the habits and habitats of each of the animals on your list and try to determine which are most likely to be predators and which are most likely to be prey of the predators. How and why are predators and prey important to nature's food chain?

Project to Pursue

Write the letters of the alphabet from A to Z vertically on a sheet of paper. Beside each letter, write the name of an animal whose name begins with that letter. When you have finished, try to categorize the animals on your list in at least three different ways.

From Border to Border _____ ICEBREAKER 65

The first person to cross the United States by automobile was Dr. H. Nelson Jackson. The venturesome motorist was a physician practicing in Burlington, VT. He embarked on his ambitious adventure in San Francisco in 1903. After crossing the nation with his "border to border" travels he brought his history-making journey to a successful close with a safe arrival back in Vermont. Quite a feat, indeed, for a motorist so early in the history of the automobile.

Point to Ponder

How would Dr. Nelson Jackson's journey compare to a journey by car today from California to Vermont?

Project to Pursue

Taking into account the condition of highways, lack of facilities (lodging, fuel stations, food stores, etc.), and limited means of communication, sketch a pictorial list of supplies and equipment Dr. Jackson would have needed for his journey.

Frozen Foods and Supermarkets ____ ICEBREAKER 66

Although we take frozen foods and supermarkets for granted, they are relatively new phenomena. The first supermarkets opened up in the United States during the 1930s. They have often put smaller stores out of business because they can offer more goods for cheaper prices. Frozen foods for the home were a creation of Clarence Birdseye. He was fishing in a frozen lake one day in the 1920s when he saw that his catch was freezing hard on the ice. He said to himself, "Why not freeze fresh fish and sell it?" Freezing foods soon became a widespread practice because the faster food is frozen, the better it tastes, and the longer it keeps.

Point to Ponder

Before people had freezers, they stored winter ice in stone icehouses and iceboxes. Imagine how your life would be different today without supermarkets and frozen foods or refrigeration. How would your shopping and eating habits change?

Project to Pursue

Lots of supermarket products come in bags and boxes. Design an unusual paper bag for a supermarket chain that is informative and creative in its color and message. Design an unusual frozen food package that contains a new frozen dessert for sale.

Giants

Giants have been popular characters in fairy tales all over the world for many centuries. Giants are people who are enormous (gigantic) in size and awesome in strength, but usually have little intelligence. Giants also tend to have overdeveloped senses, especially the sense of smell. Personalities of giants vary depending upon the culture. English giants are evil; Welsh giants are clever; Irish giants are pleasant. The best part about giants as literary characters is the fact that size never outwits cunning.

Point to Ponder

Think about fairy tales or folklore that you have read or heard about as a child. Which fairy tale could best be rewritten with the main character as a giant.

Project to Pursue

Write an original fairy tale that has a giant as its main character. What new twist can you give your setting, your plot, or your protagonist/antagonist?

The Goddess Aphrodite

It has been said that the Greek goddess, Aphrodite, was the most beautiful goddess of all. As goddess of love she had power over the hearts of mortal men and women. There are many stories about her origin ranging from reports that she was the daughter of Zeus to reports that she rose from the sea-foam near Cyprus. Everyone, however, agreed about her beauty and her reputation as "the fairest" of them all.

Point to Ponder

Elaborate on each of the following statements: (1) Beauty is in the eye of the beholder; and (2) Beauty is only skin deep.

Project to Pursue

Think about what beauty means to you. Make a list of people, places, and things that you think are truly beautiful. Compare your list with other students in the class.

Going for the Gold _____ ICEBREAKER 69

"There's gold in the river! Gold in the river! Gold, I tell you!" The shouts rang out through the streets of San Francisco on a fateful day in 1848. "Gold, you say? Real gold?" "Where? How far? How do I get there?" came the replies. From then on, people from all walks of life—some hungry for adventure, some looking for a new life in the booming west, and some just plain greedy—came from all directions to seek their fame and fortune. Some were successful; most were not. One thing was sure. Overnight, the city of San Francisco which originally began as a mission built largely by Native Americans, Spanish explorers, and priests became a boom town, never to be the same as before the great gold rush.

Point to Ponder

1. How do you think life changed for the people living in San Francisco before the gold rush? Do you think the changes in their lives were for the better or worse?
2. Is gold as valuable today as it was in 1848? What influence do you think synthetic products have had on how people in the United States value natural products such as gold, silver, and copper?

Project to Pursue

Write a short poem or ballad about some phase of the California Gold Rush.

Graphs that Tell a Story _____ ICEBREAKER 70

Graphs are important information tools for recording numbers to show how they interface. Specifically, a graph is a diagram drawn on a grid that shows how two or more sets of information are related. A line graph has two axes. The vertical axis points upward, and the horizontal axis is drawn from left to right. A bar graph is made up of vertical and horizontal bars. A circle graph has various lines radiating from its center to points along the circumference of the circle. The size of the wedges is in proportion to the size of the numbers being represented.

Point to Ponder

Think about the types of information that are best represented by graphs. Then reflect on whether line graphs, bar graphs, or circle graphs are easiest for you to interpret or develop. Finally, determine whether you are more like a line graph, bar graph, or circle graph, and why.

Project to Pursue

A graph can tell a story. Create a line, bar, or circle graph to present information on a topic or subject of your choice. Then construct a set of questions whose answers will tell your story.

The Great Captain Cook _____ ICEBREAKER 71

One of the great navigators and explorers of the new world was Captain James Cook. He is given credit for exploring the coasts of Newfoundland and Labrador, leading an expedition to the South Pacific, sailing around New Zealand and Australia, and discovering the Easter Islands of Hawaii. His greatest achievement, however, was finding the Northwest Passage, which is a route that connects the Atlantic with the Pacific. He eventually reached the North American coast by way of Vancouver and went north as far as the Bering Straits until he was blocked by ice.

Point to Ponder

Decide on the most important qualifications that were required of the early navigators and explorers. Determine whether today's navigators and explorers of outer space require the same kinds of skills and character traits.

Project to Pursue

Create a classified Help Wanted Ad for your local newspaper, recruiting both an explorer of yesterday and an explorer of tomorrow. How will they be alike and how will they be different?

Hear! Hear! _____ ICEBREAKER 72

The ear is one of the most interesting and crucial parts of the body. Without it, people and animals alike would be unable to communicate. It's interesting to note that the largest ears in the world belong to the African elephant. Bat ears work like radar to warn bats of obstacles to avoid when flying into a dark cave. Crickets listen through tiny ear slits on their front skins. Alligator ears are protected by flaps of skin just behind the eyes. Human beings hear from two ears, one on each side of the head. How well human beings learn to use these two ears can be a determining factor in their perception of and reaction to people and daily life.

Point to Ponder

Are you a good listener?

Project to Pursue

Rate yourself on a scale of 1 to 4 as to your ability to listen attentively, appreciatively, and analytically. Use the results of your rating scale to determine when and under what circumstances you use each type of listening skill during a typical day.

Henry David Thoreau

Henry David Thoreau is probably best known for his publication of *Walden*, which is a report on his hermitlike life at Walden Pond. The point of his experiment was to prove that a person could live a life of self-sufficiency away from other people and thereby escape the evils of the commercial world. He lived in a house built with his own hands, ate vegetables from the garden he planted, and supplemented his diet by fishing and hunting. He made the very little money needed for survival by doing occasional odd jobs. During his two years at Walden Pond he spent much of his time observing nature, reading, and writing. The work which has become an American classic is actually an account of one individual's conflict with his world and of his struggle to live by his own rules and avoid the complexities enforced by society.

Point to Ponder

How do you think Thoreau's two years at Walden Pond influenced the lives of those closest to him at the time? How do you think they influenced the rest of his life?

Project to Pursue

Pretend that you had the opportunity to live for a much briefer time than two years as a self-sufficient hermit in the woods. Write a journal account of your life for one typical twenty-four hour period.

Henry Ford and the Model T

Henry Ford marked the birth of the automobile industry in 1908 when he introduced the assembly line concept into his Detroit factory for the construction of the Model T. The car was mass-produced at a low cost by advancing along a production line from worker to worker as each individual performed his or her assigned task to each car. This system allowed Ford to produce many cars quickly and cheaply so that even workers who built them could afford to buy them as well.

Point to Ponder

Auto workers who built cars on an assembly line made a good salary and learned a single skill in producing a car very well. There were, however, some problems with this type of work which required that the individual do the same task in the same way on the same make of car day after day. What do you think some of these problems might be for both the workers and the plant owner?

Project to Pursue

Organize an assembly line with a small group of friends to construct a simple object with no more than five or six steps to its construction. Consider making a book mark, a paper airplane, a toy, or a piece of origami. Assign jobs to specific individuals and mass produce a large number of the objects to experience mass production firsthand!

A High Flying Flag _____ ICEBREAKER 75

In 1818, the Congress of the United States of America decreed that a national flag should be made to include thirteen stripes to represent the original states and a star to represent each state in the union. Betsy Ross, a seamstress at the time, has often been given credit for making the first flag. Many historians say, however, that even though Betsy Ross did make many flags, the credit for making the first flag still belongs to an undetermined flag maker.

Point to Ponder

If you were asked to design a new flag for the United States that would celebrate the nation's multiculturalism, what elements would you include?

Project to Pursue

Through the years the American flag has been referred to as "Old Glory," "The Red, White, and Blue," and "Stars and Stripes." Think of another name for the flag and use it as the title of a poem or short essay honoring the flag.

Homework Hassle _____ ICEBREAKER 76

Most parents want to help their children with homework assignments, but many are not certain about how they should offer assistance, especially when their children begin the more difficult courses offered at the middle school level. Research shows that children benefit when parents are involved in their education, and this includes help with homework tasks. Many students incorrectly believe that teachers do not want them to discuss homework at home and many parents incorrectly believe that they do not have the expertise to help students with the more complex assignments. One solution to this dilemma, suggested by Joyce Epstein and Karen Salinas of John Hopkins University, is to make homework assignments more interactive and to put students in charge of their homework by showing them how to guide the family discussions needed to complete their work.

Point to Ponder

Talk with a group of friends and decide what makes an effective homework assignment for you and what makes a poor homework assignment for you. Try to give specific examples to support your choices.

Project to Pursue

Create an ideal homework assignment for something you are currently studying in a math, science, or social studies class. Try to make it an interactive task that involves family members in its successful completion.

Home Workshop _____ ICEBREAKER 77

With the advances in technology, increased communication, and the need for flexibility, the workday for a large number of people is shifting dramatically. In many instances, it is no longer mandatory for large groups of workers to gather in huge skyscraper offices in congested urban settings. The electronic cottage-industry concept makes it possible for some people to set up a home workshop utilizing a computer, facsimile machine, and teleconferencing equipment in order to conduct their business or profession in an orderly manner. This opens the door to flexibility and creativity in career lifestyles.

Point to Ponder

If advances in communication and technology continue at the rate they have over the past decade, what new developments can you predict that would allow people in the future to live and work at even greater distances from their clients and/or coworkers?

Project to Pursue

Consider the advantages and disadvantages of home workplaces as opposed to traditional office settings. Develop a position paper supporting the one you would prefer if you were entering the work world today.

How Honduras Got Its Name _____ ICEBREAKER 78

Did you know that Christopher Columbus first landed on Cape Honduras on the coast of Caribbean Honduras in 1502? And did you know that this was the first place on the American mainland that he set foot? Honduras is bordered by Guatemala, El Salvador, and Nicaragua. The small, mountainous, wedge-shaped area was given its name by Spanish sailors. Honduras means "depths" in Spanish. The reason for this name was that shallow water was difficult for sailors to find, thus causing problems when they sought to anchor ships off its shores. Honduras is rich in history, culture, ancient art, Mayan ruins, and natural resources.

Point to Ponder

How would the face of history have been changed if Columbus and his party had decided to settle permanently in Honduras and discontinue their voyages of exploration to the new world?

Project to Pursue

Make up a brand-new name for your own country. Base the name on some piece of factual history, geography, or folklore associated with the discovery of your country. Weave a story around the origin of the name.

Icebergs _____ ICEBREAKER 79

The largest icebergs in the world are those that break away from Antarctica. The largest ever seen was over 12,000 square miles. The tallest icebergs break away from Greenland, and one was reported to be 548 feet above the water. The very tall Arctic icebergs are the most dangerous because eight-ninths of the ice is hidden beneath the sea. Icebergs gradually melt from the sun and warmer water as they float away from the polar lands. Waves and rain erode them further.

Point to Ponder

The great ship *Titanic* was sunk by an iceberg that had broken loose and drifted into the shipping channels or routes of the busy North Atlantic. Discuss what the people on the *Titanic* must have gone through when they realized their unsinkable ship was going down and many of them with it.

Project to Pursue

Use the following ten words in an original story about the *Titanic's* disaster: iceberg, Arctic, polar, sea, currents, channel, ocean, erosion, latitude, and temperature.

Idioms Are Intriguing _____ ICEBREAKER 80

Idioms are expressions or sayings that are used figuratively to add interest to one's speaking or writing vocabulary. They are not meant to be taken literally since they are usually made up of words that can be easily misunderstood by people looking for hard and fast meanings. They may, on the other hand, add color and interest to language or literature when used with imagination and discretion.

Point to Ponder

1. Why would it be important to avoid the use of idioms in conversation with a person just learning to use English as a second language?
2. What do each of the following idioms mean?
   a. She has a heart of gold.
   b. He is worth his weight in gold.
   c. New friends are silver. Old friends are gold.
   d. America's streets are paved in gold.

Project to Pursue

Create an original idiom to convey the following meanings:
1. Hard work and honesty will pay off.
2. Friendships are more valuable than money.
3. Lying and cheating will bring grief and shame.
4. Attitude is more important than ability.

The Infamous Al Capone _____ ICEBREAKER 81

Al Capone was a notorious gang boss who led organized crime in Chicago during the 1920s and 30s. When the government banned the sale of alcohol, illegal breweries and drinking clubs sprang up in most American cities. These bars were controlled by mobs referred to as the "Mafia," which was a secret organization made up mainly of Italian "family gangs." Al Capone is especially remembered for his ruthless killings during the St. Valentine's Day Massacre. The Federal Bureau of Investigation, better known as the FBI, was set up by the U.S. government to fight organized crime and people like Al Capone.

Point to Ponder

Discuss why gangs have become so widespread and important among teenagers today, not only in the United States but also in many cities worldwide. What makes gangs attractive to young people and what can be done about the violence so often connected with gang activity?

Project to Pursue

Create a WANTED Poster for the arrest of Al Capone that might have appeared in Chicago during the 1920s and '30s.

Is Anyone There? _____ ICEBREAKER 82

It's not unusual in today's high-tech world for a person to send a fax to someone they have never met or spoken to in response to a recorded message taken from an answering machine or voice mail. This impersonal form of communication may be between two complete strangers living in different cities, countries, or even continents. It may be between people of any age, race, or creed. It may continue until a business deal is concluded, a personal relationship is cemented, or an information base is established.

Point to Ponder

1. What influence do you think high-tech communications are having on world peace?
2. If the use of faxes, E-mail, voice mail, computer internets, and other electronic means of communication continues to grow at the same rate over the next few years, will the traditional postal system become extinct?

Project to Pursue

Some people feel that high-tech communication is causing more detachment and less attention to opportunity for the development of meaningful personal relationships. React to this feeling and write a brief paragraph giving an example from your personal experience to support your reaction.

It's All to Your Credit _____ ICEBREAKER 83

Credit means many things to many people. To a bookkeeper, credit refers to an item of income earned by a business. To a customer, credit is an arrangement he or she makes to pay for goods or services sometime after the items have been acquired. To a credit bureau, credit is information collected on a person's credit rating. To a creditor, credit represents money owed to him or her by somebody who has taken out a loan. Credit cards are an important part of business transactions today. The bank that issues the credit card pays the store the amount of money the cardholder has spent. Then the cardholder is billed by the bank once a month. If the cardholder doesn't pay his or her balance in full, he or she is charged interest for the loan.

Point to Ponder

Credit and credit cards can be both beneficial and harmful to individuals and businesses in today's world. Discuss ways that credit can be abused by people and ways that credit can enrich one's life.

Project to Pursue

Try playing the Good News/Bad News game. To do this, write out two related sentences. In the first sentence, tell the good news. In the second sentence, tell the bad news. Make your sentence pairs relate to credit.

EXAMPLE: The good news is that I charged a new skateboard to my parents.
The bad news is that my parents don't know about it.

It's a Rocky World _____ ICEBREAKER 84

The world has three different types of rock. Rocks can be classified as metamorphic, sedimentary, or igneous rocks. Metamorphic rocks are those that underwent a series of sudden changes in their structure. Marble is an example. Sedimentary rocks are formed when streams carry sediment that has eroded from the land to the bottom of the sea. Constant pressure mixes and hardens these layers, creating sedimentary rock. Sandstone is an example. Igneous rocks are formed by active volcanoes that shoot out molten material. Once this material contacts the surface of the earth, it cools and solidifies, forming igneous rocks. Basalt is an example.

Point to Ponder

Decide what each of these "rocky" expressions might mean:
1. It is going to be a "rocky road" to the championships.
2. She can't decide what to do because she finds herself "between a rock and a hard place."
3. They are as strong as the rock of Gibraltar.

Project to Pursue

The sale of pet rocks was a popular fad during the 1970s, and they were purchased by thousands of children and adults alike. Design a pamphlet telling others how to take care of a pet rock.

Japan: A Land of People _____ ICEBREAKER 85

Japan is made up of 4,000 islands populated by almost 123 million people, making it one of the most densely populated countries in the world. There are approximately 847 people for every square mile in Japan. Most of Japan's people live in the towns and cities. There are eleven cities that have populations of more than a million. Tokyo, the capital and the largest city, suffers from urban sprawl and overpopulation.

Point to Ponder

What factors do you think account for the heavy concentration of Japan's population in the cities and towns as opposed to more rural areas? How do you think this impacts the country's economy?

Project to Pursue

Compare Japan's dense population to Canada's population of fewer than eight people per square mile. Summarize the influence you think population would have on personal and professional motivations and expectations and on the rate of immigration to and from the two countries.

Junk Mail _____ ICEBREAKER 86

Junk mail has become a normal part of life today through post offices, letter boxes, and even faxes. Considering the international and worldwide emphasis on conserving and protecting the earth's natural resources and the heavy toll that the production of paper products takes on these diminishing resources, it is amazing that junk mail continues to flourish. Advertisements, solicitations, and political, financial, and charitable entreaties continue to bombard mailboxes and communication networks of people of all ages, stages, and means. While an occasional piece of junk mail may be of interest to the recipient, some is offensive, embarrassing, and an unwanted nuisance to be dealt with.

Point to Ponder

Think of some ways junk mail pieces might be recycled and put to good use.

Project to Pursue

Prepare an argument to persuade postal authorities to charge a full first-class fee for all junk mail and to eliminate bulk mail privileges for advertisements and solicitations.

Just the Facts, Please _____ ICEBREAKER 87

A newspaper article is a written report of an event told by the reporter as accurately as possible. It differs from an editorial in that there is no room for opinions, ideas, or speculations. The news reporter must learn to write clearly, concisely, and above all, factually. The successful reporter gathers the facts and then orders them in a manner to present them to the reader as clearly as possible. Readers can test the reporter's "savvy" by determining if the "five important Ws"—who, what, when, where, and why—are immediately evident in the article.

Point to Ponder

Are daily newspapers as important as a means of global communication as they were fifty years ago? How do daily newspapers influence the global economy and provide opportunities for people around the world to understand common economic needs?

Project to Pursue

Select a topic of high interest to your community and write an article appropriate for your local newspaper. Rewrite the article in the form of an editorial to present your feelings and or opinions about the subject.

Learning about Your Body Suit _____ ICEBREAKER 88

The main jobs of the skin are to protect one's internal organs from drying up and harmful bacteria from getting inside. The average person has a total of six pounds of skin that varies in thickness from 2 to 6 millimeters, and most people shed 40 pounds of skin in a lifetime. Some amazing things about this skin are that it is so flexible that you can bend and stretch it; it feels different sensations because it has nerves; it heals itself when wounded; it keeps heat in on cold days and releases it through sweat on hot days. It is a watertight container for your entire body.

Point to Ponder

Explain what you think is meant by each of these expressions:
1. Beauty is only skin deep.
2. He is a thin-skinned or thick-skinned person.
3. Let's go skinny dipping.
4. My mother is going to skin me alive.

Project to Pursue

Write an episode for a new soap opera series entitled *It's No Skin Off My Back*.

Leonardo da Vinci _____ ICEBREAKER 89

Like many highly gifted people, Leonardo da Vinci was talented in many different areas. In addition to his marvelous paintings he was a sculptor, musician, engineer, and architect. Da Vinci was born in Vinci, Italy, where he began painting and drawing at a very early age. He was a keen observer of nature and science. Many of his experiments and observations were recorded in journals. An interesting thing about these journal entries was that they were recorded in mirror writing. Leonardo da Vinci is best remembered for his painting, *Mona Lisa*, which is one of the most famous paintings in the world.

Point to Ponder

How do you think da Vinci's left-handedness influenced his work as a sculptor and painter?

Project to Pursue

Some people felt that Leonardo da Vinci used mirror writing to record his observations because of his left-handedness. Others speculated that he used this method of writing to keep his observations secret. Develop your own code to use to preserve your most secret thoughts. Write out the alphabet from A to Z. Hold it in front of a mirror and copy out the reversed alphabet. Use your code to write a journal entry related to your feelings about the contributions of great artists to world history.

A Letter Is Better _____ ICEBREAKER 90

It has been said that "a letter to a friend is a gift of one's self." In a friendly letter, one person can share thoughts, feelings, and insights about life with another friend. When this kind of exchange takes place, both friends' lives are enriched. Much of history, literature, and legend has had its genesis in letters from one friend to another. Feuds have been started and peace treaties signed because of a letter's contents. Pen pals who met for the first time after years of letter writing (or who never meet) have become lifelong friends. Couples who became acquainted and fell in love through their letters have married and built their lives together. Friends and family separated in childhood have maintained long and fruitful relationships through their letters to each other. Holding an unopened envelope in your hand, recognizing the handwriting as that of a friend, and anticipating the message inside is one of life's treats, isn't it?

Point to Ponder

Some people feel that letter writing is a dying art that will be replaced by electronic means of communication. What do you think?

Project to Pursue

Write a letter to a friend or family member who would like to know what's happening in your life. Bring them up to date on your feelings, events, and dreams. When you finish the letter you may even know more about yourself. Mail your letter!

Looking at the Land ICEBREAKER 91

The four different shapes of land forms that cover about thirty percent of the earth's surface have been caused by natural forces at work over the ages. Mountains are the highest of all, hills are next in height, plateaus are raised areas of flat land, and plains are large areas of mostly level land. Heat and pressure can cause changes in the earth's surface by raising or lowering the land and by moving large portions of land from one place to another. Wind, water, and ice can also cause changes in the earth's surface. All through history, people have made choices about where and how they live based on these land forms. Therefore, you could say that the land forms themselves have played an important part in shaping the history of the world.

Point to Ponder

Determine if your community is built on land that primarily consists of mountains, hills, plains, or plateaus. Once this determination is made, decide on how the land form influences the type of buildings you see, the jobs people have, and the overall economic stability of the community.

Project to Pursue

Elaborate on the statement, "Geography has, to a large extent, driven the course of world history." Give specific examples of heavily populated areas of the world and tell why so many people have established homes and sought gainful employment there.

Copyright ©1996 by Incentive Publications, Inc., Nashville, TN.

Look! No Hands! ICEBREAKER 92

Soccer is a most unusual game that has retained its popularity throughout the ages. Great team work and attention to individual responsibility make the game intensely interesting for both participants and spectators. Players of this world-famous sport need to be good on their feet. Twenty-two players, half of them aiming to kick an inflated ball into a goal at one end of the field, the other half aiming at the other end, engage in an aggressive competition requiring skill and strategy. After all the kicking, it is up to each team's goalie to defend the goal and prevent the other team from scoring.

Point to Ponder

Do you think that soccer is equally popular with boys as it is with girls? Do you think it is more popular in urban or rural areas? How do you think soccer rates in popularity on a national basis with softball and/or baseball?

Project to Pursue

Make up a brand-new game involving two teams, a ball, and a playing field. Let your imagination soar as you name the game and develop its rules.

Copyright ©1996 by Incentive Publications, Inc., Nashville, TN.

Lottery Madness

Lotteries have become very popular throughout the United States and Europe today. A lottery is a way of raising money by selling numbered tickets. Numbers, or a series of numbers, are drawn at random, and holders of the winning tickets receive a prize or a sum of money. Any game in which the winner is picked at random is a kind of lottery. The more lottery tickets that are sold for a given event, the less chance one has of winning the prize.

Point to Ponder

Why do people spend their money for lottery tickets? Is this considered a form of gambling? How does it compare with slot machines in casinos and bingo games in community centers? When would you buy or not buy a lottery ticket? What are your chances for winning in most lottery situations?

Project to Pursue

Pretend you have been asked to raise money for the purchase of books in your media center. Design a lottery event that could be used for this purpose. Give details for people who would be interested in supporting this lottery cause!

The Mad Hatters

In the 1890s, it was the fashion for ladies to always wear hats out in public. Most of these hats had very wide brims which were impractical and annoying because anyone sitting next to them or talking close to them would bump against them, causing embarrassment and discomfort for both parties. The hats were held in place by long, sharp pins (known as hat pins), which were stuck through the hat and the hair. The hat pin could also be used as a weapon against an unwelcome suitor.

Point to Ponder

Historically, men and women wore hats most of the time to social gatherings, concerts, church, celebrations, weddings, and even while driving or walking around town. Today hats are very seldom worn except in special circumstances. Give reasons why the wearing of hats should once again become the proper fashion.

Project to Pursue

Create a colorful and innovative hat design for a specific event or celebration that appeals to you.

The Magic of Martial Arts _____ ICEBREAKER 95

Many students today enjoy learning about the martial arts, such as judo, karate, aikido, sumo, and kendo. The martial arts are methods of self-defense and combat which began in Japan around the end of the nineteenth century. Judo is a type of jacket wrestling, while sumo is a belt wrestling sport. Karate is a way of fighting without weapons, while aikido is a system of self-defense designed to subdue the opponent. Kendo is a form of fencing done with bamboo swords so as not to hurt the participants.

Point to Ponder

Think of reasons why so many young people in this generation are turning to the martial arts as a hobby or special interest area.

Project to Pursue

Karate is a popular form of self-defense today. Learn a few basic karate moves from a book on karate or a friend who has taken lessons. Think about what you would do if you were in a situation where you needed to defend yourself. Should you learn one of the martial arts?

Majestic Mexico _____ ICEBREAKER 96

Mexico, with its mountains, deserts, jungles, beaches, modern cities, rural villages, and small towns, has been called a land of contrasts. From the hustle and bustle, traffic jams, and skyscrapers of the big cities to rural settlements where the pace of life is much the same as it was centuries ago, Mexico remains one of the world's most colorful countries. The beautiful beaches, magnificent scenery, churches, and marketplaces attract many visitors to Mexico. Concerts, arts, festivals, and fiestas honoring patron saints contribute to Mexico's reputation as a tourist attraction destined to please even the most jaded tourist.

Point to Ponder

Think about how life has changed for the Mexican Indian tribes since the early Spanish settlers arrived there. How much of their original culture do you think they have been able to retain?

Project to Pursue

Piñatas are decorated containers usually made of papier-mâché and are to be filled with goodies for special occasions. Blindfolded children scramble to break the piñata with a long stick in order to claim the goodies as part of the holiday celebration. Sketch a piñata, complete with Mexican decorations, that you would like to make.

Many Offbeat Uses for Everyday Products

Many times we buy products for the single use "touted" on the container or package of the product. Surprisingly, inventors behind many of these products have actually developed multiple uses for them which are little known to the consumer. Did you know that petroleum jelly can lubricate roller skates and skateboard wheels as well as remove chewing gum from hair? Did you know that lemon juice can be used as an invisible ink for writing secret messages and to get rid of dandruff? Finally, did you know that salt can soften a new pair of jeans in the washing machine and can keep slugs away from the house?

Point to Ponder

Think of reasons why a manufacturer of a product would focus on a single use of a product rather than promote and advertise its multiple uses.

Project to Pursue

Think of other household products that might be used for multiple purposes and suggest alternative uses for them.

Media Mania

The old style middle school library with books lining every wall and a card catalog to provide easy access to every book in the collection is quickly fading from the scene. Students entering middle schools today are more apt to find a media center equipped with a plethora of multimedia equipment including (but not limited to) books, magazines, newspapers, computers, televisions, and radios. Instead of requiring students to remain seated and maintain complete silence, librarians and teachers should encourage students to move from center to center, develop cooperative learning groups, and work interactively with teachers and students.

Point to Ponder

Do you think the move to multimedia centers from libraries whose main resources were limited to books will result in students reading fewer books and being less avid readers? Give reasons for your answer.

Project to Pursue

Develop a check list to use in evaluating your school's library or media center. Be as specific as possible in defining the criteria to be used in determining its qualifications as a true multimedia laboratory for learning.

Meet the Shadow
ICEBREAKER **99**

A shadow is simply a dark area produced by a solid mass which intercepts the many rays emitted by a light source and blocks their passage. Shade is linked to light and will vary in color according to the color of the light producing it. If an object is lit by a beam of white light, the shadow cast by it will be black; if, however, we use a beam of red light, the color of the shadow will be blue. In the same way, green light will give a magenta shadow and violet light a yellow one. If three colored lights are switched on at the same time, there will be shadows of different colors.

Point to Ponder

In your own words, explain how shadows are made outside. Give examples of common shadow patterns which you are likely to see on the playground or inside the school itself. What type of weather is most likely to produce shadows?

Project to Pursue

Many years ago before television was invented, there was a very popular radio show called *The Shadow* that many people loved and listened to each week. The Shadow was a male figure who appeared at certain times to prevent acts of crime and violence to innocent victims. Nobody ever saw his face or knew who he was. Write a short script for one of these broadcasts featuring the Shadow.

Copyright ©1996 by Incentive Publications, Inc., Nashville, TN.

Metamorphosis
ICEBREAKER **100**

Some creatures, such as the butterfly or the frog, undergo several internal and/or external changes as they grow from a baby to an adult. When the egg of a butterfly hatches, for example, a little grub or larva appears and goes through three basic stages called the larva stage, the pupa or chrysalis stage, and the adult stage. Before it can look like its beautiful mother, the grub has to change its appearance, undergoing a complete transformation called metamorphosis. The frog, on the other hand, goes from a life that is aquatic to one that is terrestrial. From an egg, the tadpole hatches and resembles a tiny fish that breathes through its gills. As the tadpole grows, its gills become smaller and its back legs and forelegs develop. The tail then disappears and the frog climbs out of the water as an adult creature who will spend the rest of its life both on land and in the water.

Point to Ponder

If you could transform yourself through a metamorphosis, what would you want to become?

Project to Pursue

Design a congratulatory greeting card that could be sent to an adult butterfly or frog who has undergone metamorphosis.

Copyright ©1996 by Incentive Publications, Inc., Nashville, TN.

Microwaves Take Over _____ ICEBREAKER 101

As you might expect, the microwave oven gets its name from the rays that cook the food, which are called microwaves. They penetrate into the food in such a way that the food cooks on the inside first. People like to use microwave ovens because they cook (or defrost) foods very rapidly.

Point to Ponder

Determine how microwave ovens have affected each of the following: fast food restaurants, frozen food manufacturers, home kitchens, and producers of oven appliances and cookware.

Project to Pursue

Check a microwave cookbook out of the library, and prepare a meal for yourself cooking only with the microwave.

The Mighty Jag _____ ICEBREAKER 102

"Here it comes!"
"There it goes!"
"Going, going, almost gone!"

No, we're not talking about the automobile. Even though the car is also sleek, speedy, and rare, the mighty jaguar of the animal kingdom is the one in danger of extinction. The jaguar population is being diminished at an alarming rate by hunters who kill the animal for its beautiful coat, which commands a great price in the fashion marketplace. The survival of the jaguar is further endangered by the continuous destruction of its habitat as the rain forests are destroyed.

Point to Ponder

Some people have no conviction about saving endangered species. What do you suppose is their reasoning?

Project to Pursue

Write a radio or TV commercial to discourage consumers from buying coats made from endangered animals, or design a newspaper ad to promote public support for protection of the world's rain forests.

Migrations

Many species migrate to warmer climates when the weather turns colder. Some animals travel great distances during the course of a year. The champion migrant is the stern. This bird, which spends its summers near the North Pole, flies across almost half the earth, stopping near the South Pole. Some other migratory animals that travel for many miles are the willow warbler which travels 8,000 miles each year, the gray whale which travels 5,000 miles each year, and the monarch butterfly which travels 1,800 miles each year.

Point to Ponder

People migrate over long distances when it is important to their personal safety, their religious or political beliefs, their economic welfare, or their desired lifestyles. Think about the different groups of people throughout history who have migrated to various parts of the world for better and more meaningful existences.

Project to Pursue

Write a short story about the travels of a stern, a warbler, a gray whale, or a monarch butterfly. Tell what it sees, what it does, and what it learns as a result of this annual journey from one place to another.

Military Slang

Many Americans have chosen a career in the military. These people and their families move often and get to live in many different parts of the world. They live on military bases that serve as small, self-contained communities. The military service has its own form of slang which includes such terms as: (1) Army Brat = young child of army personnel; (2) Big Boot = the general; (3) Company = a recruit; (4) Spud Call = call for kitchen work; (5) Jack = money; (6) GI Lemonade = water; (7) Come on the Green = challenge to fight; and (8) PX = stores for shopping.

Point to Ponder

Think about the advantages and disadvantages of pursuing a career in the armed forces.

Project to Pursue

Prepare a set of questions you might want to ask the "military brat" of a career officer.

The Miracle of the Nile _____ ICEBREAKER 105

The Nile is the longest river in the world. It flows over 4,000 miles from the mountains of east and central Africa to the Mediterranean Sea. On its journey it wanders through deserts, rock, sand, and swamps. It flows past villages which look very much as they did in Biblical times, as well as cities offering modern amenities and attractions. Through the ages the Nile has held a mystery and magic of its own for travelers from around the world who come to marvel at the rich culture and remnants of the great civilization made possible by the life-giving waters of the Nile.

Point to Ponder

Why has the Nile been romanticized through the ages by writers, sculptors, painters, and musicians?

Project to Pursue

In your own words write the definition for each of the following: Egyptologist, pyramid, exploration, archaeologist, archaeological dig.

Money Matters _____ ICEBREAKER 106

"A penny saved is a penny earned."
"A fool and his money are soon parted."

Point to Ponder

"Begin early to take care of your pennies and the dollars will take care of themselves." How does this quote relate to students as they look to the future?

Project to Pursue

Read the above quotations carefully and ponder the meaning each one has for you. Agree or disagree with the message they convey about saving money. Support your position with three good statements. Create a new quotation to convey your own feeling about saving money. Compose a jingle, rap, or song to convey your message in a manner that will capture the people's interest.

Music Makes the World Go Around _____ ICEBREAKER 107

Eric Salzman said that "there is music for everybody." Music, sounds played or sung together having rhythm, melody, or harmony, is an important part of our lives. Through the advent of the compact disc and high-tech worldwide communications, we have incredible access to all kinds of music. At the touch of a finger we can hear opera, classical music, rock and roll, church music, spirituals, the blues, progressive alternative, folk music, country music, and pop music. What is your favorite kind of music? Take some time to listen and find out.

Point to Ponder

Imagine that music disappeared from our lives. Think about all the things that would no longer exist because they are dependent on music for their survival.

Project to Pursue

Ask your parents to loan you some unique music, perhaps classical, opera, or folk music. Write a paragraph on how it makes you feel. If you truly enjoy this type of music bring it in to share with classmates or friends.

The Mystery of the Dead Sea _____ ICEBREAKER 108

The Dead Sea is five times as salty as the world's oceans. The shores of this saltiest body of water also mark the lowest point on the earth's land surface. The Dead Sea measures 49 miles in length. It is approximately ten miles wide at its deepest part. The water is so full of salt and other materials that it is almost impossible for a swimmer to sink. There is little aquatic life in this salty sea.

Point to Ponder

In your own words, explain how the Dead Sea got its name.

Project to Pursue

Invent a sea creature who thrives in salt water and loves living in the Dead Sea.

News on the Line _____ ICEBREAKER 109

Newspapers have been a regular part of daily life for people all over the world for many years. They have been looked to as the source of news not only about world and local happenings, but also about education, sports, entertainment, comics, agriculture, home and gardens, religion, food, finance, and much more. In today's world of electronic transmission, many people are turning to TV and/or radio news broadcasts, talk shows and special coverage of live events, and the Internet for this same information. Speculation as to how much longer large daily newspapers will be considered a vital and influential part of the world communication system is a topic of great concern to publishers, investors, employees, and advertisers of the giant newspaper empires.

Point to Ponder

Rank from 1 to 4 (with 4 being the highest) the following list as it applies to your source of information for daily news: daily newspaper, radio, television, internet.

Project to Pursue

Outline a panel discussion related to examination of the advantages, disadvantages, and possible consequences of the demise of the daily newspaper. Support your outline with ten good questions to be answered by knowledgeable panel members to be drawn from both newspaper and other media professions.

A Number of Animals _____ ICEBREAKER 110

Animals are fascinating creatures to study for many reasons, the least of which is unusual things about them that can be expressed by numbers. Did you know that a lobster has ten legs, a jellyfish is 95% water, a sperm whale has a brain that weighs 20 pounds, a hummingbird often visits 200 flowers a day, a mayfly has a lifespan of about two hours, a midge insect beats its wings 62,000 times a minute, a seahorse lays 400 eggs at a time, and a tapeworm may grow up to 40 feet long with up to 3,000 segments?

Point to Ponder

Think about ways you might explain these number facts to a young child who doesn't yet understand such concepts as percents, pounds, feet, minutes, hours, or whole numbers in multiples of ten.

Project to Pursue

Make up a mathematical word problem for each of these animal number facts. Try to use each operation (addition, subtraction, multiplication, and division) at least once in your set of problems.

The Number One State _____ ICEBREAKER 111

Delaware, whose capital is Dover, has every right to be called the number one state of the United States of America. Bordered by Maryland, Pennsylvania, and New Jersey, it is the only state that has a "rounded" border. Before the approval of the United States Constitution, three flags flew over Delaware. They were the Dutch, Swedish, and finally the English flag. On December 7, 1787, Delaware acquired the historic honor of becoming the first state to be admitted to the union of the United States of America.

Point to Ponder

Philadelphia, Pennsylvania, the nation's first capital, was replaced by Washington, D.C., in 1800. Speculate on how the development of the nation would have been different if the decision had been made to designate Dover, DE, as the capital city of the then-young nation. What, if any, influence would the geographic location of Dover have had on the government?

Project to Pursue

Pretend that you were a teenager living in Delaware on the day that it was admitted to the union as the first state. Write a journal entry to reflect your feelings about the historic event.

Numbers and Number Systems _____ ICEBREAKER 112

A numeral is a symbol that stands for a number. Numerals are grouped in various ways to make a numbering system that helps people to make calculations and solve number-related problems. People have written numerals in multiple ways as these symbols vary from culture to culture. Numerals can also be written as number words. The following words represent the numbers 1 through 10 for the Japanese culture:

1 = ichi	4 = shi	7 = shichi	10 = ju
2 = ni	5 = go	8 = hachi	
3 = sa	6 = rokun	9 = ku	

Point to Ponder

Many people feel that the numeral *0* and the number word *zero* tend to have negative connotations or interpretations. People think that *zero* means nothing, nobody, or zilch. Think about as many positive ways as you can to describe the meaning and/or importance of zero in our lives. How has it been used in meaningful ways?

Project to Pursue

Use the Japanese numbers from one to ten to construct a series of word problems. Provide an answer key for your work.

One Giant Step _____ ICEBREAKER 113

"That's one small step for man, one giant leap for mankind."
These were the words uttered by the American astronaut who, in July 1969, became the first human being to set foot on the moon. After that fateful day, boys and girls around the world would no longer say "maybe I'll be the first person on the moon." The man on the moon had become a real person named Neil Armstrong. All of the hard work of scientists, engineers, and technicians, the vast financial resources, long hours, and bravery of flight crews and astronauts had paid off. Space exploration had triumphed with "one giant leap for mankind" and the world would never be quite the same again.

Point to Ponder

How do you think the accomplishments of the early astronauts have influenced the course of world history? What influences have they had on career options available to people your age?

Project to Pursue

Predict how space exploration will continue to change the lives of human beings over the next century. Create a comic strip, cartoon, or series of sketches to portray your predictions.

On Top of the World _____ ICEBREAKER 114

The region around the north pole known as the Arctic is a fascinating part of the world that is well worth learning about. Arctic lands include parts of Alaska, Canada, Norway, Sweden, Finland, Russia, Siberia, and the island of Greenland. The moss and lichen of the tundra region have unique qualities that allow them to flourish in the bleak and swampy soil where little other plant life can survive. In other parts of the Arctic, where sunlight is more prevalent for longer portions of time, berries, vegetables, and even flowers can grow. This "top of the world" location makes the area a desirable destination for scientists, explorers, photographers, writers, and adventurers who come to study the exotic flora and fauna of the region as well as for anthropologists and social scientists interested in the history and lifestyles of its human population. Forests of spruce, fur, and pine as well as birch, maple, and other trees grow in certain areas. Fish are abundant, and there are vast mineral resources, including coal, gold, and copper. Whales, porpoises, walruses, reindeer, musk ox, ermine, and sable also inhabit this cold, stark area of the world.

Point to Ponder

If you could go on an expedition to the Arctic what particular aspect of the region would you be most interested in studying?

Project to Pursue

Justify the need for a scientific expedition to the Arctic region by listing ten good reasons for continued exploration.

Ordinary Products with Extraordinary Uses

ICEBREAKER **115**

Some products, such as cola drinks, toothpaste, yogurt, and oatmeal, have some little-known, practical uses for their products that are unusual and effective. Colas can be used to clean a toilet bowl or remove rust spots from chrome car bumpers. Toothpaste can be used to dry up acne pimples and remove crayon marks from walls. Yogurt can be used to soothe sunburn pain and canker sores. Finally, oatmeal can be used to relieve itching from chicken pox and to give yourself a dry shampoo.

Point to Ponder

Think about each of the uses for the products described here and give reasons why you think each of them is effective in these ways.

Project to Pursue

Create a colorful magazine advertisement for one of the above products promoting its unusual applications rather than its traditional uses.

The Origin of Ice Cream

ICEBREAKER **116**

Did you know that ice cream originated in the Orient? The great explorer Marco Polo saw people eating it there and brought the idea back to Italy. It spread to France and became so popular that the nobility tried to keep the secret for making ice cream from the common people. Ice cream is made of cream, milk or milk solids, sugar, and sometimes eggs. Vanilla, chocolate, berries, fruit ingredients, and nuts are added as flavors. A stabilizer is added to retain the smoothness of the ice cream by preventing the formation of coarse ice crystals.

Point to Ponder

Defend or dispute the idea that ice cream is the most popular dessert in the world. Be specific in your arguments.

Project to Pursue

Invent a new ice cream flavor. Name it, describe it, and draw a picture of it.

Parasitic Worms _____ ICEBREAKER **117**

Flatworms and round worms are invertebrate animals which are parasitic in nature and possess qualities that are harmful to our health. The effect that these worms can have on plant and animal life is of such significance that a special branch of parasitology has been established to study them in order to combat infectious disease. Flatworms have bodies that are flattened like ribbons. They live in water or moist places. Three kinds of flatworms are planarians, flukes, and tapeworms. Flukes and tapeworms are parasites which live inside other organisms. Roundworms are round, threadlike worms which can live anywhere, although most live in water or in the soil. Roundworms are one of the simplest animals to have a complete digestive system.

Point to Ponder

Compare and contrast the long-range effects of these animal parasites with plant parasites such as mistletoe and mosses that live on trees and the choking vines that cover bushes, shrubs, and other plants.

Project to Pursue

Make a list of questions you would ask a parasitologist expert about the habits and effects of parasitic worms in your own community.

The Passage of Time _____ ICEBREAKER **118**

Did you know that a year is determined by the time it takes for the earth to make one complete revolution around the sun? A calendar year is 365 days, while a solar or tropical year is actually 365 days, 5 hours, 48 minutes, and 46 seconds. Leap year occurs every 4 years when all the extra hours, minutes, and seconds of the solar year are added up to make an extra day. We date each year according to its relation to the year of Christ's birth. To indicate this relation, we use the abbreviations B.C., meaning "before Christ," and A.D., meaning "anno Domini," Latin for "year of our Lord."

Point to Ponder

Defend or dispute the idea that time is a person's most valuable resource. Think about how time might be viewed differently by a preschooler, a teenager, an adult parent, and a senior citizen.

Project to Pursue

Write a short response to each of these "time-related" statements that begin with the words *I WONDER WHAT IT WOULD BE LIKE TO . . .*
1. Go back in time and live in a previous historical period.
2. Be 150 years old.
3. Invent a time machine.
4. See myself at some time in the future.

A Passion for Picasso _____

Picasso was a famous Spanish artist who is probably the most celebrated painter of the twentieth century artists. His earliest paintings were dominated by the color blue, which depicted the poverty he saw around him in Barcelona. In his mid-career, he moved to Paris to work with another painter, Georges Braque, on a new style of art known as cubism. Cubism shows figures as fragments of geometric shapes and is very colorful and imaginative.

Point to Ponder

Think about the color blue and describe the many things that you associate with this color. Does blue conjure up more sad images than happy images? Explain.

Project to Pursue

Create an original picture using only geometric shapes. Make it colorful, vibrant, and imaginative.

The Phenomenon of_____
Stalactites and Stalagmites

The water that filters through the roof of a cave is rich in a mineral called lime carbonate. Over many years, the drops of water filtering through the cracks in the ceiling deposit the lime carbonate. Eventually, as the water evaporates, the deposits solidify and form a kind of stone icicle called a stalactite. Stalagmites are formed the same way, except that the mineral solidifies on the ground. Sometimes stalagmites and stalactites grow until they come together and form columns.

Point to Ponder

Explain why you think so many people are fascinated by caves and often spend time and money visiting them throughout the world.

Project to Pursue

Create a simple advertising brochure for a new tourist attraction called "The Caves." Show what the caves look like, complete with multiple stalactites and stalagmites. Include a bat or two because the bat is the only kind of mammal that lives in the biggest caves, clinging to the walls.

Photosynthesis

Would you believe that plants, like people, need to eat, but they feast on sunshine instead of pizza through a process called photosynthesis? The photosynthesis cycle has five steps.

1. Air containing carbon dioxide enters the plant through the leaves.
2. Water from the soil travels through the roots and stems of the plant to the leaves.
3. Chlorophyll in the leaves absorbs sunlight.
4. Water breaks up into hydrogen and oxygen, and oxygen is given off to the air through the stomata of the leaves.
5. Chemical reactions in the plant then produce a simple form of sugar, called glucose, that is either used right away as food or converted to starch and stored in the plant for use at a later time.

Point to Ponder

If you were to give special awards to plants, which of them would receive the following blue ribbons? Largest plant, smallest plant, most beautiful plant, ugliest plant, fastest growing plant, slowest growing plant, easiest plant to care for, and most difficult plant to care for.

Project to Pursue

Think of as many words as you can from the letters in the word "photosynthesis." All of your words must be at least four letters long. Write these words out in alphabetical order.

Plants on the Table

More and more of the world's food supply is coming from plants. This is partially due to the fact that many people are becoming vegetarians. Even in early times, some physicians prescribed a diet based only on plants to improve their patients' health. These diets were often supplemented by herbs or other plant materials as cures for specific diseases. Modern health food stores and herb shops support the same type of healing powers by offering not only the old standbys but also many new plant derivatives that have been laboratory-tested for their health-giving properties. Animal-rights activists' opposition to killing animals for food has also contributed to the move toward vegetarian lifestyles.

Point to Ponder

Compare a vegetarian diet with one including meat. Consider health, convenience, economy, taste, and other factors. Which do you think is better?

Project to Pursue

Create a vegetarian lunch that you would be proud to serve to your friends to celebrate a special occasion.

The Pleasures of Plastics

In our society today, plastics are used everyday in a wide variety of ways. They can be soft or hard, rigid or flexible, clear or colored. Plastics are used to make everything from containers, luggage, and videotapes to tableware, cloth, paints, and glues.

Point to Ponder

Speculate as to what you think plastic does to the environment. How does the use of plastic, for example, save on the cutting down of trees? How does the use of plastic, on the other hand, impact landfills and recycling efforts?

Project to Pursue

Think of ten different uses for each of the following plastic items: plastic squeeze bottles of dish detergent, plastic rings for packaging soft drink cans, plastic silverware for picnics, and plastic covers for jar containers.

The Plunder of Pirates

Pirates were called robbers of the high seas; they attacked ships, plundering and stealing their goods and treasures. Piracy was a frequent practice in the Mediterranean during the Middle Ages. By the nineteenth century piracy had almost disappeared except for some places in Indonesia. The Barbary Coast was a true pirate state set up in North Africa during the sixteenth century. Interestingly, pirates were regulated by written rules, which established a rigorous discipline to be followed by all on board the ship. It was not unusual for a pirate to be punished for an infraction with "forty stripes minus one on the bare back," according to Moses' law.

Point to Ponder

Today many amateur sailors traveling for pleasure on their sailboats in the Caribbean Sea are being stalked, robbed, and killed by drug dealers in cigarette boats. Discuss how this is a form of piracy on the high seas similar to the early practices in the Mediterranean.

Project to Pursue

Construct a list of rules and punishments for pirates that might have been written during the sixteenth century. Record these on a scroll-type document.

Predators and Prey _____

The balance in nature depends in part upon successful relationships between predators and prey. A predator is an animal that attacks and kills other animals for food. All of the animal world is organized into a type of food chain, in which animals prey on other animals and are in turn preyed upon themselves. Animals have many different types of adaptations and specializations to help them trap their prey or escape their predators. Some animals are adapted to run swiftly but silently; others chase their prey in packs, like wolves, and attack their victim as a group.

Point to Ponder

Think about predator and prey relationships among people. Are there human beings who prey on the weaknesses and frailties of other people and/or other cultures? On the other hand, how can a vulnerable person protect him- or herself from people in power?

Project to Pursue

Think of several different predator and prey scenarios in the animal world. Act out several of these situations and see if others can guess what creatures you are portraying.

The Pyramid of Egyptian Society ___

The social structure of ancient Egypt was a kind of pyramid. At the top was the pharaoh who ruled the kingdom. Just below him were the priests and the noblemen. The priests were to keep the gods happy through prayers and sacrifices and to teach reading and writing to scribes. Below this rank were the soldiers who also enjoyed great prestige. Next came the middle class of merchants and craftsmen who provided the much needed goods and services for the culture. On the bottom half of the pyramid were the workers and peasants who toiled in the fields and farms along the Nile. Most peasants were free citizens unlike the slaves who, at the very bottom of the pyramid, were assigned to domestic work and work in the mines.

Point to Ponder

Historians often describe ancient Egypt and the life of the pharaoh as a colorful and glamorous period in the history of early civilization. Think about what your life would be like if you were a member of the pyramid of Egyptian society.

Project to Pursue

Compose a short diary entry for a particular event that could have taken place around 3100 B.C. in an Egyptian community. Write about this event from the perspective of the pharaoh, a priest, a soldier, a merchant, a peasant, and a slave. How might their viewpoints differ?

Quotable Quotes

Victory at all cost, victory in spite of all terror,
victory however long and hard the road may be;
for without victory there is no survival.

Winston Churchill, prime minister of Great Britain during World War II, used these words to encourage the English to fight against the Germans to the end. He knew that they had no choice, and he did much throughout the war to encourage his people.

Point to Ponder

What would you do if you were in a position where there was no survival without victory? Would you be brave enough to keep fighting and never give up? What impact would have been made upon Great Britain today if they had surrendered to the Germans?

Project to Pursue

Look up some more famous quotes from Winston Churchill. How do you think he influenced the outcome of World War II?

Quotes Worthy of Note

William Shakespeare's famous quotations have lived through the ages as words to use and ponder by people of all ages and all walks of life. Shakespeare is often referred to as the world's greatest dramatist, and he is probably the most renowned English poet. His variety of characters as well as the richness of his settings and plots distinguish his work. In his writing, he drew from his vast knowledge of music, the Bible, art, law, military science, sports, animal husbandry, and more. Shakespeare's works are as popular today as they were in his time because of his marvelous use of the English language. Many lines spoken by his characters encompass the thoughts and feelings of the human spirit so that they speak to people throughout the ages.

Point to Ponder

Copy the following quote on a sheet of paper. Relate to it and create a quote of your own to convey a comparable message. "What's in a name? That which we call a rose by any other name would smell as sweet" (*Romeo and Juliet,* Act II, ii, 43-44).

Project to Pursue

Reflect on this quotation and reflect on what it means to you in relation to your personal life: "He jests at scars that never felt a wound" (*Romeo and Juliet,* Act II, ii, 1).

Reasons for Rainbows _____ ICEBREAKER **129**

Rainbows form when sunlight passes through millions of raindrops. The light is bent as it enters each drop, then bent once again as it leaves the drop. This bending motion causes the white sunlight to separate into its seven separate colors. Each color hits your eye from a slightly different angle, and you see a rainbow. When a rainbow forms, the order of the colors is always red at the top, then orange, yellow, green, blue, indigo, and violet at the bottom. Rainbows are beautiful arcs of color!

Point to Ponder

Folklore would have us believe that there is a magic golden pot at the end of every rainbow. If this were true, think of ten different things you would want to find in that special pot the next time you are lucky enough to see a rainbow.

Project to Pursue

Create a design for wallpaper, wrapping paper, stationery, or fabric that features a rainbow as part of its pattern.

Resources for References and Research _____ ICEBREAKER **130**

Today students have many different resources to use as reference or research tools. These can be found in most school and public libraries and are often available in both print and electronic formats. The atlas is a book of maps. A biographical index is a book of important facts about famous people. A dictionary is a book of words listed in alphabetical order that includes multiple definitions, spellings, and pronunciations. An encyclopedia is a book that contains information on every subject arranged in alphabetical order. A gazetteer is a geographical dictionary or index with the names and locations of places also arranged in alphabetical order. A thesaurus is a book of words with their identified synonyms. An almanac is a book of the most current information on a wide range of timely topics.

Point to Ponder

If you had to list the above references according to their importance to you in getting your school work done, how would your list be arranged?

Project to Pursue

Create a display to promote and sell your number one reference tool!

The Road Less Traveled _____ ICEBREAKER 131

Robert Frost was an American poet whose works have become an important part of American literature. It's interesting to note that while he is most often looked upon as a rural poet, writing about the New England countryside and lifestyle in which he grew up, his first works were actually published while he was living in England. One of the reasons that his writing holds such a universal appeal is the simplicity and conversational nature of his writing style. While reading the works of Robert Frost, one almost feels as if the poet himself were in the same room speaking directly to the reader. Despite the poem's simplicity, the messages conveyed in Frost's writings are meaningful and memorable and more profound than is at first apparent. One of his most famous poems is "The Road Not Taken."

Point to Ponder

An often-heard statement is "he or she is marching to his or her own drummer." Do you think this is possible without loosing step with the band?

Project to Pursue

Elaborate on the statement "Life is full of trade-offs" as it applies to each of the following:
Your life at the present time   Your family
School policies   Your national government

Robert Louis Stevenson _____ ICEBREAKER 132

Robert Louis Stevenson was the author of such diverse works as the well-known books *Treasure Island* and *A Child's Garden of Verses,* as well as many other books of fiction, poems, and essays. He is one of few writers whose works have remained popular through the years with both young children and adults. Robert Louis Stevenson can truly be called a great storyteller because of his constant attention to maintaining the interest of the reader through use of description, strong plots, and lively characters. Born in Edinburgh, Scotland, he continued to write throughout his life in spite of living the life of a wanderer, seeking cures for his poor health. In later life, he moved to Samoa with his family. He lived there and was active in politics and government until his death.

Point to Ponder

How do you think Robert Louis Stevenson would conduct his search for health today? How could modern technology and advances in medical science be of help to him?

Project to Pursue

Make a list of questions about the life and works of Robert Louis Stevenson. List the resources you would use to find these answers.

Safari Surprises

Safaris are trips made by groups of people to hunt or watch wild animals found in places such as East Africa. Over the years hunters and farmers have killed so many animals that some species are now endangered. The most famous safari parks include one in Kenya and one in Tanzania. People go there with their cameras rather than guns to shoot pictures instead of bullets at the wildlife. Poachers, however, still pose a threat to some animals, such as elephants, who are slaughtered for their valuable tusks.

Point to Ponder

Decide whether or not you would like to go on a safari. Where and when would you want to go and who would you want to accompany you?

Project to Pursue

Write a detailed description of a wild animal that one might see on a safari in East Africa. Without naming your animal, try to describe it while someone attempts to draw it from your words.

Sandro Botticelli

Sandro Botticelli's real name was Allesandro di Mariano di Vanni Filipepi. He adopted the name Botticelli from his brother's nickname. The literal meaning of Botticelli was "little barrel." Botticelli had his own workshop in his native Florence by the age of twenty-five. Botticelli is best known for his paintings with religious subjects and for his portrayal of ancient Greek and Roman myths. In many of his works, he used a circular shape and actually painted the figures to "follow the circle." He painted for churches, for his patron who was a member of the famous Medici family, and even for the Pope.

Point to Ponder

Botticelli's works are representative of the Renaissance period in which he lived and worked. Renaissance means rebirth. As you think about a period of rebirth, what exciting possibilities come to mind? What would you like to see take place during a renaissance period in your own country right now?

Project to Pursue

Write a myth or a story about a heroic event that you would like to see memorialized in a circular-style painting comparable to Botticelli's style. Single out the scenery, characters, or details from your myth that should be included in the painting.

Save the Rain Forests _____ ICEBREAKER 135

It's easy sometimes for people living in urban areas such as New York City, Hong Kong, Paris, and Toronto to forget human beings' dependence on many taken-for-granted benefits of the world's rain forests. Despite being home to some of the world's most endangered animals and helping to control worldwide climates, the rain forests continue to be destroyed to satisfy demands by consumers.

Point to Ponder
1. How are the world's climate and water cycles being affected by the destruction of the rain forests?
2. What kind of substitutions could be made for the (so highly prized) exotic woods taken from the rain forests?

Project to Pursue
List three specific things people can do to help save the world's rain forests.

Sea Cliffs and _____ ICEBREAKER 136
Dune-Covered Beaches

When you read travel brochures, listen to songs about the romance of Massachusetts's Cape Cod, or hear visitors home from vacation rave about its beauties, it's hard to remember that those sandy beaches were made possible by high piles of rocks and sand pushed into place by a glacier traveling more than twelve thousand years ago! When the glacier melted, the remaining debris was shaped into the cape by wind, weather, and ocean. This region is now a coveted destination for writers, artists, and tourists from all over the world, who come to enjoy the ambience of daily life as well as the sea cliffs and dune-covered beaches.

Point to Ponder
Compare and contrast the aftereffects of a glacier, an iceberg, and an avalanche.

Project to Pursue
Sketch a picture postcard and a message to send to a friend from your pretend-vacation to Cape Cod.

Setting a Good Example _____ ICEBREAKER 137

People will always follow a good example; be the one to set a good example,
then it won't be long before the others follow. . . . How lovely to think that no
one need wait a moment, we can start now, start slowly changing the world!
How lovely that everyone, great and small, can make their contribution toward
introducing justice straightaway. . . . And you can always, always give
something, even if it is only kindness!

– Anne Frank

Point to Ponder

Do you agree or disagree with Anne Frank's statement, "How lovely that everyone great
and small, can make their contribution toward introducing justice straightaway"?

Project to Pursue

Make a list of ten people you admire for the good examples they set for others to follow.
Beside each person's name list the trait or behavior you most admire (honesty, concern for
others, hard work, etc.). When your list is complete, underline the three traits that you
would most like for others to see in you.

Signs and Symbols _____ ICEBREAKER 138

Mathematics is a type of language with its own special words and signs or symbols that stand for
those words. Signs and symbols are quicker to write than words and have universal definitions.
Visual learners often enjoy mathematics because they find signs and symbols effective ways to learn
new concepts. Many mathematical signs and symbols are also used in business and commerce. Some
of these are the signs or symbols for dollar, cent, at, and account.

Point to Ponder

Think about all of the mathematical signs and symbols that you have learned to use over the
years in school. How many of these signs or symbols do you know: plus or positive, minus or
negative, multiplied by, divided by, equal to, equivalent to, less than, greater than, perpendicular
to, parallel to, ratio sign, degree, foot or feet, inch or inches, therefore, pi, and square root?

Project to Pursue

Many years ago people identified their family and heritage with coats of arms. Families would sew
these on flags and banners. Knights would paint them on their shields. These pictures or symbols
were used to convey "big ideas" that had universal meanings and interpretations. The coat of
arms was a source of family identity and pride. Create some pictures or symbols to represent
twenty to twenty-five key ideas of interest to you such as wisdom, loyalty, bravery, love, power,
strength, and honesty. Use some of them to create your own coat of arms.

Skyscrapers

Today's cities boast of many skyscrapers, tall buildings with many floors. The first one had ten floors and was built in Chicago in 1883. The invention of elevators in 1853 stimulated the growth of these structures to house everything from banks to businesses. The tallest building in the United States is the Sears Tower in Chicago, while one of the tallest buildings in Europe today is the Eiffel Tower in Paris.

Point to Ponder

In the book *From the Mixed Up Files of Mrs. Basil E. Frankweiler*, two children run away from home and hide in a famous art museum. If you had to spend the night in a famous public building someplace in the world, where would you want to stay and what would you plan to do?

Project to Pursue

Survey the students in your class to determine the tallest building they have ever been in. Graph your results.

Slithery Snakes

The snake is certainly not most people's favorite animal. The fact that many snakes are deadly, poisonous creatures only serves to make them more exotic and worthy of study. Their characteristics, habitats, and habits provide background material for a wide variety of scientific study, folklore, and speculation. While snakes are cold-blooded animals, they are not slimy like the eel and earthworm but are dry and smooth with a cover made of scales which are really folds in the skin. Snakes are deaf and their eyes are protected by a transparent cap that is shed with their skin. No one knows if snakes ever sleep because their eyes are constantly open. Their long, forked tongue is actually harmless. One interesting fact about snakes is that some are hatched from eggs while others are born alive like mammals. Contrary to popular belief, most snakes are not poisonous, but it is safe to say that enough snakes are poisonous to make it most expedient for the uninformed person to stay out of their way.

Point to Ponder

What do people mean when they say "he speaks with a forked tongue"?

Project to Pursue

Use this springboard to create an original story. "Right there, on the steps of the school, I spotted a huge snake, curled and ready to strike . . ."

The Small but Beautiful _____ ICEBREAKER 141
Hummingbird

Hummingbirds are among the most interesting of all the world's birds. Full-sized hummingbirds weigh just about as much as a copper penny. If this sounds strange, just think about the fact that an average nest is about the size of half a walnut shell and holds two eggs which, when hatched, produce baby hummingbirds about the size of bumblebees. In spite of their size, these tiny birds come equipped with some powerful tools for survival. A long tongue that can be quickly withdrawn, swiftly moving wings that allow it to remain suspended in the air, and the ability to fly straight up much like a helicopter are just some of the hummingbird's amazing traits.

Point to Ponder

As you think about the tiny hummingbird and its ability to survive in a world of predators, recall some other living creatures with special features that allow them to protect themselves from danger and possible extinction. Marvel again at nature's many wonders.

Project to Pursue

Visualize a hummingbird that is suspended before a flower, using its extended tongue, or flying straight up into the air. Sketch the picture you see in your mind and write a short poem about it.

The Social Ant _____ ICEBREAKER 142

The ant is one of the most social animals. As a matter of fact, ants are distinguished among all insects for their ability to live and work together and their natural instinct to help one another. Ants living in a common colony share both work and food. Ant colonies closely resemble communities established by human beings. Ants are very industrious and are able to build nests and survive in environments that would be impossible for most insects to inhabit. They are not highly selective about what they eat and have proven their ability to adapt to their surroundings. Some species of ants actually invite other insects into their nests where they feed, protect, and make pets of them.

Point to Ponder

What are the most important lessons to be learned from studying the history, habitats, and habits of ants? How could you best learn more about ants?

Project to Pursue

Just for fun, visualize ant cities made up of small, humble nests inhabited by modestly successful ants, high-rise condominiums populated by career workers on their way "up," mansions for the wealthy, and every level of housing between the extremes. Sketch your imaginary "ant city."

Speaking of Spices_____ ICEBREAKER 143

Since earliest history, spices have been highly prized for their contribution to food and health as well as for their pleasant aromas. Poets, artists, and musicians have extolled their virtues; diets and "miracle cures" have been based on them; businesses have flourished; and explorers have discovered new lands while searching for them. Spices are derived from plant sources as diverse as seeds, roots, bark, leaves, bulbs, fruit, and flowers. While gathering and packaging herbs and spices for sale is big business, the home herb garden continues to be both a hobby and a food source for people in all parts of the world.

Point to Ponder

Why were spices so prized by people living in times before the availability of refrigeration and other modern means of preserving food?

Project to Pursue

List as many herbs and spices as you can think of. Create a new recipe using one or more of the spices as an important ingredient.

The Special Dandelion_____ ICEBREAKER 144

The dandelion, with its yellow flowers in spring and its downy fluff in summer, is one of the few popular weeds. Its "fluff" contains the seeds which, carried by the wind, can fall to the ground many miles away from the mother plant. During the winter, the seeds remain where they fall only to germinate in the spring and grow into small plants with leaves arranged like a rosette around a flower bud in the summer. As the summer wears on, the flowers slowly change to the downy seed-bearing fluff, with autumn bringing the cycle to a close. The dandelions wither and die, having lived their entire life in the space of one year.

Point to Ponder

Think about what would happen if the lifespan for human beings was only one year. How would they do things differently than they do now?

Project to Pursue

The sunflower, unlike the dandelion, has become a popular design for articles of clothing, for hair ribbons and hats, for napkins and stationery, and for dishes and pottery. Pretend you are a designer of products for a new line of merchandise in a department store using the dandelion as your major motif. Create a series of drawings to show unusual items for sale that celebrate this popular weed!

Stories in Pictures

Some say it is hard to determine if William Hogarth is best remembered as a painter or storyteller. In either case, it is fair to say that this multitalented individual was a master of both. As the son of a London school teacher, William Hogarth spent much time as a youngster pursuing his natural interest in drawing. He became well-known first for his portraits and later for his paintings and engravings that gave detailed portrayals of everyday life. Many of these works featured evils to society such as greed and negligence. One of the techniques that distinguished William Hogarth's paintings was the use of lines and space to create interesting crosshatched designs.

Point to Ponder

Consider the quote "a picture is worth a thousand words." What is your reaction to it?

Project to Pursue

Use pencil lines of varying thickness, spacing, and shading to portray a feeling or emotion (example: anger, grief, joy, excitement, etc.). Ask a friend to identify the emotion and explain the rationale you used. Share and discuss your concept with your friend.

Storybook Characters

Some books are said to be classics and are read by children of many generations. Classic stories or tales have a special appeal because they are timeless, well-written, creative, unusual, and fun to read. Classics come in all different sizes and shapes, with a wide variety of characters, plots, settings, and points of view. Some classical titles were written many years ago while others are more recent. It is important for students to become familiar with these classics because literature is an important means for transferring one's culture.

Point to Ponder

Think about each of these famous storybook characters and try to identify the title of the book for each one: Alice, Charlie, Charlotte, Claudia, Dorothy, Eloise, Fudge, Hans Brinker, Harriet, Laura, Mafatu, Pippi, Mr. Popper, and Tom.

Project to Pursue

Choose one of the characters listed above, and write a letter to him or her stating what you like best about his or her role in the story or book.

The Suffragettes _____ ICEBREAKER 147

Many years ago, women could not vote. Campaigns for women's suffrage (right to vote) began in earnest about 1848 in the United States and in 1865 in Great Britain. The name "suffragettes" was given to women who took militant action in support of women's suffrage. Sometimes women had to go on hunger strikes, go to prison, or give speeches on street corners in order to get the public's attention. In 1920, the United States gave all women the right to vote, while Great Britain did so in 1928.

Point to Ponder

Think of as many reasons as you can why you think women were not allowed to vote prior to the early 1920s.

Project to Pursue

Skywriting is a popular form of sending political and marketing messages to the people. Think of several "sky messages" that could have been sent by the suffragettes and write them using a sky motif.

Superstitions in Sports _____ ICEBREAKER 148

Most amateur and professional athletes acknowledge the fact that there are several superstitions associated with their respective sports which are taken seriously by the players. It is important for fans to know what these are so they can avoid bringing bad luck to their favorite teams. Some of these include:

- In baseball, lending a bat to a fellow player is a serious jinx
- In basketball, bouncing the ball before taking a foul shot brings good luck
- In football, a mascot is an important good luck symbol
- In tennis, it is bad luck to wear yellow
- In bowling, to continue a winning streak, wear the same clothes
- In fishing, spit on your bait before casting your rod to make fish bite
- In golf, start only with odd-numbered clubs
- In ice hockey, it is bad luck for hockey sticks to lie crossed

Point to Ponder

Debate reasons why some people are superstitious and some people are not. What makes the difference?

Project to Pursue

Think of a new use for each of the following sports items: home plate, basketball hoop, football helmet, tennis racket, bowling pin, fishing rod, golf club, and hockey puck.

Swimming Upstream _____ ICEBREAKER 149

The Pacific salmon intrigues people because of its most unusual habit of leaving the ocean to return to the stream of its birth to reproduce. To do this, the salmon must swim upstream, battling raging waters and swift waterfalls to reach the quieter inland streams. More fascinating and poignant, however, is the fact that after this great effort the salmon dies. Its mysterious urge to dive headlong into the stream in this manner leaves much for scientists to learn about the habits of the many species of salmon. One thing we do know is that people the world over recognize salmon as a major source of food. Its unique flavor and availability have been spread immeasurably because its quality and flavor can be preserved and the salmon can be shipped in tin cans to all parts of the world.

Point to Ponder

What does the term "swimming upstream" mean to you? Have you ever found yourself in a situation where you felt that you were "swimming upstream"? How did you handle it?

Project to Pursue

Canned salmon continues to provide tasty meals for campers, soldiers, explorers, and other people without access to kitchen facilities. Create a tasty recipe for using canned salmon as the main course at a dinner during an outdoor excursion you would like to take with a group of friends.

Symbols Say a Lot _____ ICEBREAKER 150

Each of the fifty states that make up the United States of America has its own state flag, tree, bird, and flower. Families have a family crest, companies have a company logo, towns and cities have flags, sports teams and schools have emblems or nicknames, and many other institutions and groups have adopted some symbol that they feel appropriate to represent them to the rest of the world. These symbols help build awareness of the unique features of the group and build pride as they provide a unifying spirit. Throughout history, symbols have been important elements of the development and progress of civilization as we know it today.

Point to Ponder

1. Do you know what your state flower, tree, and bird are?
2. Do you know if your town or city has a flag and/or symbol or logo?
   If your answer to either of these questions was "no," try to find out more about each one.

Project to Pursue

Think carefully about the unique features of your school: its location, student population, and special strengths. Design a school flag representative of all of these.

Take Off on Tessellations _____ ICEBREAKER 151

A Dutch artist named M. C. Escher combined mathematics and art to create tessellations that have become well-known and respected by mathematicians, artists, and people of all ages and from all walks of life. The Webster's dictionary defines tessellations as "mosaic; especially a covering of an infinite geometric plane without gaps or overlaps by congruent plane figures of one type or a few types." Many of M. C. Escher's designs have served as the inspiration for clothing, games, puzzles, decorative objects, and other commercially produced products. These products are most often found in museum shops, specialty shops, and catalogs.

Point to Ponder

How will the study and use of tessellations help to prepare students for the study of geometry?

Project to Pursue

Design an original tessellation to be used as a jigsaw puzzle. Cut it into the most interesting puzzle pieces possible. Put the puzzle pieces in an envelope and on the outside of the envelope. Exchange puzzles and work them.

Take Time to Find Out _____ ICEBREAKER 152
What I Am Thinking, Please!

One way to get to know someone better is to ask interactive questions that promote dialogue. There are hundreds of questions and activities that can serve as catalysts for discovering what is special about another human being. A person has to practice both active questioning and active listening skills if he or she is going to be an effective communicator.

Point to Ponder

How can you tell when someone is really interested in you? How can you tell when someone is really listening to you? How can you tell when someone is really communicating with you?

Project to Pursue

Work with a small group of friends and try using one or more of these questions to engage one another in a meaningful dialogue. Remember to practice your active listening skills in this exercise.
1. If you could have magical powers, what would they be?
2. What kind of things really upset you?
3. If you could ride on a flying carpet, where would you go?
4. If you could be one age for the rest of your life, what age would you like to be?
5. Do things that happen on television and the movies also happen in real life? How do you know?

Talents Unlimited

People who are fortunate enough to recognize their own talents and abilities early in life have a good "head start" on the road to later successes. Many schools today offer aptitude tests and other assessment opportunities to help students learn more about themselves and their own personal strengths and weaknesses. Once talents and abilities are identified, it is important for both students and teachers to make every effort possible to provide appropriate and challenging individualized learning goals for each student.

Point to Ponder

Benjamin Franklin left us the following wise saying:
"Hide not your talents
  For use they were made.
  What's a sundial in the shade?"
How does this saying apply to you and the use you make of your own best talents?

Project to Pursue

Use a web graphic organizer with the five Ws (who, what, when, where, and why) to outline a talent show for your class. As an appendix item, add the qualifying criteria for participation and for the awards to be granted.

Tales Told and Retold

Whole histories of people, places, and events have been saved from extinction through folktales that were handed down from one generation to another. However and wherever they have been told, they have held audiences of one to thousands spellbound. They include fables, fairy tales, myths, poems, and ballads. Some folktales have lived for centuries while others have survived for only a short time. One thing they have in common is that they all seem to have a simple but captivating plot, a definitive setting, and an exciting cast of characters.

Point to Ponder

How would storytellers such as the brothers Grimm and Hans Christian Anderson fare in today's world of high tech? Would their stories be as appreciated if they were told with modern characters and situations?

Project to Pursue

Have you noticed that many of the best known fairy tales actually have no fairy in them? Take one of your favorite fairy tales with no "fairy" and rewrite it to include a mystical character such as a giant who cried giant tears, a laughing leprechaun, a cross fairy princess, a wicked troll with a forked tongue, a tiny little elf no taller than your finger, etc.

Teacher Talk

Helen Keller, who was both deaf and blind from the age of eighteen months, became a role model and image of hope for handicapped people around the world. In adult life, she became an advocate for the blind and deaf and accomplished much good for them through her writing and speaking engagements. She gave great credit for her success and ability to build a personally rewarding lifestyle to her faithful teacher, Miss Annie Sullivan. This great teacher was so devoted to her student that she remained with her as both teacher and friend for fifty years.

Point to Ponder

Does the average student truly respect and show appreciation for the teacher's extra efforts on their behalf?

Project to Pursue

Write a short essay based on the specific things that good teachers do that inspire students to do their very best work.

The Thousand and One Nights

The book *The Thousand and One Nights* is among the best known and most read collections of stories in the world. These stories, also known as *The Arabian Nights*, were first written in Arabic. Their actual origin is debatable and has added to their legendary appeal to readers throughout the ages. Many believe that the Arabians got the stories form the Persians and that the Persians took some of them from India. They were introduced in Europe in the 1700s where they were translated by a Frenchman named Galland. Since that time they have been printed in many languages, to be read and reread by people around the world. Some of the most popular stories are Ali Baba, Sinbad the Sailor, and Aladdin.

Point to Ponder

What common characteristic of *The Thousand and One Nights* has made it possible for these stories to remain popular with people of all ages and backgrounds through the years? Can you think of other stories that fall in this category?

Project to Pursue

One of the chief attractions of these stories is their portrayal of life in the Orient. Create a setting, plot, and characters for a story based on life in the Orient today. Give your story a title and make an outline for it.

Tongue Twisters

Alliteration is one type of figurative language that repeats the use of a single letter at the beginning of each word in a phrase or a sentence. Tongue twisters are short and simple alliterative lines or words that tell a story, ask a question, or make a statement. There are two rules for saying tongue twisters correctly. First, they must be said fast, and second, they need to be repeated a certain number of times. If the tongue twister is several sentences long (like the size of a paragraph), you only need to say it once. If the tongue twister is just one or two short sentences, say it twice, and if it is less than a sentence long say it three times.

Point to Ponder

Analyze the three tongue twisters below and then determine what makes them so difficult to say fast without stumbling over the pronunciation of the words. Determine what letters of the alphabet you think are most difficult to repeat in a tongue twister.

Project to Pursue

Practice saying each of these three different types of tongue twisters and then make up some of your own.
1. Can an active actor always actually act accurately?
2. A big bug bit a bold bald bear and the bold bald bear bled blood badly.
3. Three gray-green greedy geese, Feeding on a weedy piece, The piece was weedy, And the geese were greedy, Three gray-green greedy geese.

Tornado on the Way

"Tornado on the way" is a warning worth heeding. The tornado is one of the most violent of all windstorms. Even though the dark, funnel-shaped cloud covers a smaller area than most cyclonic storms, the damage it causes can be tremendous. Tornadoes usually occur in the late spring or early summer, and they form when a mass of cold air forces its way under moist, warm air. Nearly all tornadoes move in a northeasterly direction following the boundary of a cold front. They are dangerous only when they touch down to earth. Meteorologists advise people in the path of a tornado to go into a basement if possible if they live in a frame house. People living in brick or stone houses are advised to stay in a hall or closet on the ground floor since the tornado might rip the house apart and throw debris into the basement.

Point to Ponder

How much do you know about tornadoes? Would you know what to do if a tornado was coming? What would you do if you were outside?

Project to Pursue

Make a plan to detail what your class would do in the event of a tornado. Hold a tornado drill so that you and your classmates will be prepared in the event of an emergency.

The Tragedy of Pearl Harbor _____ ICEBREAKER 159

Many people will never forget the morning of December 7, 1941. Japanese bombers attacked the United States naval base at Pearl Harbor, Hawaii, completely catching the Americans off guard. The Japanese destroyed six warships, damaged twelve others, and destroyed 174 aircraft. This untimely attack took the United States into the war against Japan and its allies, Germany and Italy.

Point to Ponder

The basic cause of conflict between Japan and the United States at the time of the attack on Pearl Harbor was Japan's occupation of the French colony of Indochina, now Vietnam, Laos, and Cambodia. Not everyone alive during that invasion would view its results the same way. Assume the point of view of the following people and think about their perception of what happened and why it happened: a native resident of Hawaii, a naval officer stationed at Pearl Harbor, and a pilot for a Japanese bomber.

Project to Pursue

Create a front-page headline and feature article for an American newspaper that describes this event from history.

True Friendship _____ ICEBREAKER 160

"In the end, a person's wealth is measured more by the number of friends than by the amount of money accumulated in a lifetime."

"To have a friend, be a friend."

"A true friend is someone who knows all about you and likes you anyway."

Point to Ponder

Review your list of traits for friendship and check yourself to see how you rate as a true friend. Be honest in looking at yourself before you begin rating your three best friends.

Project to Pursue

All of the above quotations refer to friendship. Read them carefully, then decide what, if anything, they all have in common. Make a list of ten traits that you think a good friend must possess. Using a rating scale of 1 to 5 (with 5 being the highest), rate each of the traits for its importance to true friendship.

True or False

Many historians believe that the story of George Washington and the famous cherry tree may well be fiction rather than fact. In the legend, young George is supposed to have answered his father's question about who cut down a highly prized cherry tree with the response "I cannot tell a lie, Father. I cut down the cherry tree." As a result of this story, pictures of young George, hatchet in hand, clumps of cherries, and mottoes related to truth have been symbols of Washington's life. They appear in classrooms across the country each February 22nd as part of the birthday celebration honoring the first president of the United States. It is from this story also that Washington acquired a reputation for telling the truth under all circumstances.

Point to Ponder

Sometimes people may feel that the absolute truth is harmful and that what they would describe as a "situational lie" might be justified. What do you think?

Project to Pursue

Choose a person in your class to write "two truths and a lie" about. Try to capture the "true spirit" of the person with the truths and make the lie as believable as possible but absolutely not true. Ask a friend to identify the lie.

The Ups and Downs of Elevators

Elevators are important to the world of work and architecture. Without elevators, construction of buildings and locations for businesses would be very limited. The car of the elevator that carries people from one floor to another actually hangs from one end of a cable. An electric motor turns a drive pulley that winds the cable up and down. At the other end of the cable is a big weight called a counterbalance. This weight balances the weight of the car so that the motor has to raise and lower only the weight of the people inside the elevator. A safety device called a governor stops a car from falling if the cable breaks, so elevators are very safe to use.

Point to Ponder

How would our lives be different without elevators? What might actually be improved if elevators were eliminated from our lifestyles?

Project to Pursue

Write a poem, short story, or skit about the "Ups and Downs of Elevators." Can you include a special metaphor or image about elevators in your creative writing?

The Wearing of the Green _____ ICEBREAKER **163**

On March 17 most people who march in parades, attend parties, sing songs, tell jokes, and wear green to celebrate St. Patrick's Day are not particularly concerned with the factual accuracy of information concerning the holiday's origin. They much prefer the wealth of rich legends and folklore that St. Patrick's Day brings to mind. When told that St. Patrick was really from a Roman family, was raised in Britain, captured as a teenager and carried to Ireland as a slave, and was later returned to his homeland, they say, "But he did go back to Ireland where he left his heart and became a famous Irish saint." Most of them also say, "Who cares if the legend of St. Patrick chasing all the snakes out of Ireland may be just a wee bit stretched since there were no snakes in Ireland? It's the laughter, the gaiety, and the excuse for an Irish celebration that gives this holiday its claim to fame."

Point to Ponder

Think green. In three minutes, list as many green things as you can think of. Use the next three minutes to list things that once were green, but are now some other color. Where did the green go?

Project to Pursue

The Irish people are known for their humor. Draw a big shamrock. Inside the shamrock, write a humorous limerick, a jingle, an ode, or a song to recognize St. Patrick. Make sure it's humorous!

A Whale of a Tale _____ ICEBREAKER **164**

Blue whales, which may weigh as much as 300,000 pounds, are the largest animals known to man. The survival of these huge marine mammals is seriously endangered by commercial whaling, oil well drilling, and pollution. In fact, their number is decreasing so steadily that some scientists predict that there may be only 1,000 or less left today.

Point to Ponder

Why is it important to save the enormous blue whale?

Project to Pursue

Outline a multimedia project or a lesson plan complete with student work sheets to convince students to work actively and aggressively to protect the blue whale and other endangered marine animals.

What Are Dreams Made Of? _____ ICEBREAKER 165

The "content" of dreams comes from something that affects you while you are sleeping or something that haunts you from the past. All of our dreams relate to our emotions, fears, longings, wishes, needs, or memories. There are people called psychoanalysts who have made a special study of why we dream, what we dream, and what those dreams mean. Many of these analysts feel that dreams are basically expressions of wishes that didn't come true and a dream is a way of having your wish fulfilled.

Point to Ponder

Think of the many dreams you have had lately and decide whether you agree or disagree with the analysts who say that a dream is a way of having a wish fulfilled.

Project to Pursue

Write a short essay describing your special dreams, longings, and wishes for the future.

What Do You Know? _____ ICEBREAKER 166

It's easy for all of us to talk about the things we know, and sometimes we find it easy to talk about things we don't know. Maybe this sounds like a redundant statement or even like a catchy tongue twister, but it's worth thinking about. One of the phrases in the English language that many people find hard to use is the phrase "I don't know."

Point to Ponder

How will this activity help you to know more about yourself?

Project to Pursue

1. Fold a sheet of drawing paper into three folds.
2. At the top of one section write "Ten Things I Know for Sure." On the second fold write "Ten Things I Think Are True, but I'm Not Sure." On the third write "Ten Things I Don't Know but Would Like to Know."
3. Read each list carefully. Then decide: Who could you share the things you know for sure with? How could you gather information to check the things you think you know but aren't sure? To whom could you say "I don't know about this, but I'd really like your help in finding out" about each item on your "I don't know" list?

"What If" and Your Imagination ___ ICEBREAKER 167

Too often schools focus only on facts rather than fiction or on information rather than "what if" ideas. The best curriculum in a school program establishes a balance between critical-thinking skills like problem solving and decision making and creative-thinking skills like fluency and originality. It is important to learn basic facts, but it is also important to learn different ways to interpret and apply these basic facts.

Point to Ponder

Decide whether you prefer to write creative stories or factual reports and why. Are you better at writing one than the other? Do you have more opportunity to practice writing one than the other? Do you get better grades on one than the other?

Project to Pursue

Respond to each of these "WHAT IF" statements and then think up a few of your own to share with students in class:
WHAT IF MONEY EVAPORATED IF YOU DIDN'T SPEND IT WITHIN A WEEK?
WHAT IF EVERY THIRD MONTH WAS DECEMBER?
WHAT IF PEOPLE NEVER GOT SECOND CHANCES?
WHAT IF EVERYONE HAD A PLACE TO LIVE AND FOOD TO EAT?

What's Bugging You? ___ ICEBREAKER 168

Did you know that most insects that we call bugs are not really bugs at all according to the scientific definition? Bed bugs, aphids, and pond skaters are among the small group of real bugs whose scientific name is Hemiptera. These bugs all have sharp mouth parts designed to help them pierce plants and skin and suck sap or blood into their mouths. Perhaps this is why the bug has become a symbol of bothersome or destructive traits and the basis of such commonly used expressions as "he or she bugs me," "that really bugs me," and other negative expressions.

Point to Ponder

After you have completed the project below, reexamine your list carefully. Is there something you could do to "stamp out" each of the bugs?

Project to Pursue

List things that "bug you" at home or at school, and list other things that you feel strongly about. Beside each item on your list, draw a "bug" to represent your feeling. Give each bug a name and a short description. Try to make your work representative of the frustration you feel about this situation.

What's in Your Best Interest? _____ ICEBREAKER 169

Simple interest is an economic term which describes the price a lender charges when someone borrows money. Very often the lender is a bank or a loan company. Until the borrower pays back all of the money, he or she pays interest at regular intervals, perhaps each month or each quarter of the year. Compound interest is interest calculated on the amount of money originally borrowed, plus any interest that has been added to this sum. For example, if a loan is for $100 and the interest rate is 12% per year or 1% per month (12÷12), the first interest payment is calculated on $100 and will be $1. The next interest payment will be calculated on $101 ($100 plus $1 unpaid interest), and will be $1.01. Needless to say, compound interest amounts are higher than simple interest amounts.

Point to Ponder

The word *compound* is an interesting concept which can be used in a variety of contexts other than its economic application. For example, what is a compound word? What is a compound sentence? How might these words be related to the compound eye of an insect?

Project to Pursue

Make a list of questions you might like to ask both a lender and a borrower of money. Keep in mind what it means to pay interest on a loan you may want to take out to purchase something important.

What's That Smell? _____ ICEBREAKER 170

Animals have a keen sense of smell, which is one major way they gather information about their environment, their habitats, and their predators. The world's smelliest animal is an African cousin of the striped skunk which is called a zorille. The spray of a zorille can be detected half a mile away by a human, and its aroma is extremely strong and distasteful.

Point to Ponder

Discuss the difference between an odor and a fragrance.

Project to Pursue

Make a list of ten things that smell good to you and ten things that just plain stink! Rank these items from 1 to 20, with 1 being the best-smelling item and 20 being the worst-smelling item.

Next, pretend you are the curator of a modern museum that is featuring a new exhibit about smells. Briefly describe the top twenty odors that should be featured in this exhibit.

Where Are the Animal Fathers? ____ ICEBREAKER 171

Did you know that most animals never see their parents, especially their dads? This is because many insects, fish, or amphibians that hatch from fertilized eggs are expected to face life all on their own. Some animal fathers, however, do make a valuable contribution to the care of their young. A catfish father keeps the eggs in his mouth until they are ready to hatch. This takes several weeks, and he can't eat in the meantime. Father penguins withstand the intense cold of the Antarctic for 60 days to protect the eggs which he keeps on his feet covered with a feathered flap. The father sand grouse flies as far as 50 miles a day in order to soak himself in water and return to his nest, where his chicks can drink from his feathers. Finally, the father wolf guards the den of his babies and teaches them how to survive in the wild.

Point to Ponder

Decide what major roles and responsibilities human fathers should have today. Have these roles changed in the last century? If so, how and why?

Project to Pursue

Compose a thank-you note from a baby catfish, penguin, sand grouse, or wolf to his or her father that tells him how much it appreciates his role in its upbringing.

Whistler, The Painter _____ ICEBREAKER 172

Have you ever seen a reproduction of one of James Abbott McNeill Whistler's famous oil paintings? Whistler is considered one of the most notable American artists of the 1800s. His work is especially valued for its originality of style, his ability to portray the true essence of his subject matter, and his use of color. He labeled himself as a realist but retained the privilege of selecting the elements he wished to feature in each of his etchings, watercolors, oils, or lithographs. Throughout his life, Whistler defied all criticism and continued to paint his subjects in the light in which he chose to have them remembered.

Point to Ponder

Whistler's portrait of his mother is one of the world's most famous paintings and hangs today in the Louvre in Paris. Do you think it would be harder or easier for a painter to use a member of his family or circle of close friends as a model than to use a professional model? How do you think the personal relationship would influence the finished painting?

Project to Pursue

Think about the value of knowledge of art history and art appreciation. Assess the opportunities for education of this nature available to you. Write a letter to the editor of your local newspaper encouraging increased awareness and support for the arts in your community.

Who Says There Are No Rules for Wars?

In 1864, the Geneva Treaty of Switzerland developed a set of international rules for war which were accepted by all European countries, the United States, and several countries in Asia and South America. Some of these rules are: (1) warring nations cannot use chemical weapons against each other; (2) prisoners of war must be humanely treated and protected from violence; (3) killing anyone who has surrendered is prohibited; (4) zones must be set up in fighting areas to which the sick and injured can be taken for treatment; (5) the free passage of medical supplies is allowed; (6) attacks on civilians and undefended towns are prohibited; (7) any army that takes control of another country must provide food to the people in that country.

Point to Ponder

Work with a small group of friends to discuss which of these rules for war are most likely to be enforced and most likely to be abused according to your thoughts and feelings.

Project to Pursue

Rules are important for everybody to know and follow. Think of a set of rules for each of the following literary characters: Goldilocks, Pinocchio, Snow White, Cinderella, and Rumpelstiltskin.

Who Were the Neanderthals Anyway?

The Neanderthal people lived over 70,000 years ago in Europe during what is known as the Ice Age. Anthropologists have found their remains in such places as Germany, Great Britain, France, and Italy. Neanderthal people were short and muscular. They had long, low skulls with very heavy ridges over their eyes. They lived in caves and used fires to keep warm. They made stone axes and wooden spears with which to hunt mammoth and the wooly rhinoceros.

Point to Ponder

Determine whether the life of the Neanderthal people was more simple or less simple than our lives today. Consider such things as food, shelter, clothing, and health/safety issues when making your decision.

Project to Pursue

Write out a series of responses to one or more of the following "what if" statements:
1. If you could have personally witnessed one event in history, what would you want to have seen?
2. If you could have one group of people from history live their full lives over again, starting now, what group would you pick and why?
3. If one of your parents/guardians was to be a famous person from any time in history, who would you want them to be?

Wiggling through Word Problems — ICEBREAKER 175

It is important for students to learn how to solve word problems in math. Problem solving is a major life skill required in all types of jobs and careers. Word problems involve many different mathematical operations and use of terms. It is important that one read the problems carefully and then determine what math functions are needed to obtain the correct solution.

Point to Ponder

Most students find it hard to solve word problems in math. Give some reasons why you think this is true.

Project to Pursue

Make up a two-step word problem about a topic of interest to you (or find one in your math text). Analyze the stated word problem with its solution by completing several of these ideas:
- The problem was asking for . . .
- This is how I thought about the problem . . .
- This is what I tried . . .
- This is what finally worked . . .
- I couldn't figure out this problem because . . .
- I know this is the correct solution because . . .
- I found this problem easy (or hard) to solve because . . .

Wordly Wise — ICEBREAKER 176

Etymology is the study of the history and development of words. It concerns the origin of words and the way their meanings and spellings have changed throughout the years. English history reflects the growth of English words. Saxons provided the foundation and many words were later added as the Danes, Romans, and Norman French contributed words from their own vocabulary to the English language. Most dictionaries provide information on the etymology of many entry words.

Point to Ponder

How will modern technology and advanced means of communication influence the use of the English language in your own community?

Project to Pursue

Create three new words related to the growth in the use of technology in today's world. Write the pronunciation, part of speech, meaning, sample sentence, and etymology. Read your sample sentence to a friend and see if they can give you the meaning of the new word just from hearing the sentence.

A World of Color _____ ICEBREAKER 177

The four basic colors are red, blue, green, and yellow. All other hues, shades, and tints are formed from these four primary colors. Color can influence mood, attitude, and one's general sense of well-being. Some colors have been labeled cool colors and some warm colors. Many artists have painted works for long periods of time with a predominance of one color. Sometimes these works are referred to as having been painted during his or her "blue, green, red or yellow period."

Point to Ponder

Why do you think that over the years black has become a symbol of death or grief, purple a symbol of royalty, red a symbol of bravery, and white a symbol of purity?

Project to Pursue

Write a short essay on the use of color to portray feelings and/or to help meet needs of special situations. Include the following examples and give reasons for your selections:
- The color you would paint walls in a cluster of hospital rooms reserved for seriously ill patients
- An artist's studio
- Your classroom

Writing Instruments _____ ICEBREAKER 178

Over the years, people have used many different utensils for writing. These include everything from quill pens to fountain pens to ballpoint pens. Pencils also come in many different sizes, shapes, and colors. In fact, both pens and pencils are used extensively today as advertising gimmicks for businesses, as give-aways for schools, and as sale items for retail outlets.

Point to Ponder

Decide on the advantages and disadvantages of writing with a pencil, a pen, and a word processor on a computer. Determine the best use or practice for each item.

Project to Pursue

Pretend that you are a pen or a pencil and write a short essay that describes who, of all people, you would want to own and use you in their work.

You and the Environment _____ ICEBREAKER 179

Governments and industries can spend billions of dollars trying to clean up and restore the environment, but it won't be enough unless people, like you, join in the effort to minimize the effects of water, air, and noise pollution. The number of new departments, agencies, and environmental groups has greatly increased at both the state and local levels since 1970. Much of what is being done has happened because citizens have lobbied their elected officials for action.

Point to Ponder

Unfortunately, many kids and adults have little respect for their own immediate environment as they continue to litter the school grounds, the streets, the parks, the beaches, and the public places in the community. Why do people litter, and what can be done to change their "litterbug" behavior?

Project to Pursue

Write a letter to one of the Environmental Protection Agencies in your community and inquire about their activities and ask for information that you can read and distribute at the school.
or
Make a list of specific things which you and your family could do to help protect our environment for future generations.

Your Rights If Arrested _____ ICEBREAKER 180

A police officer must read a list of rights to any person who has been arrested for any crime. This list is called the "Miranda Warning" and contains the following statements and questions: (1) You have the right to remain silent and refuse to answer any questions; (2) Anything you say may be used against you in a court of law; (3) As we discuss this matter, you have a right to stop answering my questions at any time you desire; (4) You have a right to a lawyer before speaking to me, to remain silent until you can talk to him or her, and to have him or her present when you are being questioned; (5) If you want a lawyer but cannot afford one, one will be provided to you without cost; (6) Do you understand each of these rights I have explained to you? (7) Now that I have advised you of your rights, are you willing to answer my questions without an attorney present?

Point to Ponder

It has been said that the perpetrators of crime today have more rights than their victims. How do you feel about this issue?

Project to Pursue

Outline a set of plans for conducting a poll of students in your classroom regarding the rights of victims versus the rights of criminals.